TEMPLE, TOMB AND DWELLING:
EGYPTIAN ANTIQUITIES FROM THE HARER FAMILY TRUST COLLECTION

Gerry D. Scott, III

with an introduction by
Nancy Thomas

UNIVERSITY ART GALLERY
California State University, San Bernardino

FUNDERS

This exhibit is funded in part by the Instructionally Related Program Board of Associated Students, California State University, San Bernardino; the Foundation for California State University, San Bernardino; the San Bernardino County Museum; the Fine Arts Commission of the City of San Bernardino; the California Arts Council and the Harer Family Trust.

No state funds were used to print this catalogue.

Library of Congress Cataloging-in-Publication Data

Scott, Gerry D.
    Temple, tomb and dwelling : Egyptian antiquities from the Harer
Family Trust Collection / by Gerry D. Scott, III ; with an
introduction by Nancy Thomas.
       p.   cm.
  "University Art Gallery, California State University, San
Bernardino, San Bernardino County Museum.
January 8-March1, 1992."
   Includes bibliographical references.
   ISBN 0-945486-08-1 (pbk.)
   1. Egypt--Antiquities--Private collections--United States-
-Catalogs. 2. Art, Egyptian--Private collections--United States-
-Catalogs. 3. Harer, W. Benson--Archaeological collections-
-Catalogs. 4. Harer, Pamela K.--Archaeological collections-
-Catalogs. I. Thomas, Nancy, 1948- . II. California State
University, San Bernardino. University Art Gallery. III. San
Bernardino County Museum. IV. Title.
DT58.9.S36 1992
932--dc20

                               91-39824
                                  CIP

©California State University, San Bernardino 1992
ISBN 0-945486-08-1

TABLE OF CONTENTS

Foreword...iv

Acknowledgments...vii

Preface...ix

Notes to the Catalogue...xi

Chronology...xiii

Map...xv

Introduction, Temple, Tomb and Dwelling, Pt. I...1

Introduction, Temple, Tomb and Dwelling, Pt. II...128

Abbreviations and Bibliography..206

FOREWORD

The University Art Gallery, California State University, San Bernardino will be eternally grateful to Pamela and Benson Harer for allowing their collection to be shown in our Gallery. The willingness to share this enormously powerful and beautiful collection is, indeed, very generous. The visitor to the University Gallery and the San Bernardino County Museum Gallery will come away with a unique experience, better able to understand and manage his place in the history of world art and culture. My gratitude is extended to Pamela, Ben and their children on behalf of the University and the community at large.

Richard M. Johnston, Director, University Art Gallery

CSUSB University Art Gallery Harer Family Trust Exhibition Staff

Katherine P. Lintault	Assistant to the Director
Julius Kaplan	Exhibition Consultant
George McGinnis	Catalogue Design
Odette C. Salvaggio	Catalogue Design Production
M. Robert Markovich	Photographer
Steve Hopf	Photographer
Robin Kaplan	Editor
Kerry Kugelman	Preparator
Don Faust	Printer
Wyatt Portz	Color Separations

FOREWORD

The collection of Egyptian antiquities in the Harer Family Trust is one of the most significant private collections in the Inland Empire and one of the finest of its kind in the world. The Museum is pleased that the Harer family is sharing this collection and supporting this premier exhibit in the Inland area, and we are pleased to join with California State University, San Bernardino, to make its display possible.

Temple, Tomb and Dwelling is an aptly-named selection of Egyptian artifacts that reflect the splendid ceremonial practices and fascinating daily life of this ancient center of civilization. The richness and variety of the Harer family collection befits a museum setting, and the collaboration of the San Bernardino County Museum and California State University, San Bernardino, in staging the exhibit reflects our continuing commitment to making notable educational and cultural exhibits and events available to citizens and visitors to our area.

Dr. Allan D. Griesemer, Museums Director

San Bernardino County Museum Harer Family Trust Exhibit Committee

Barbara Fleming	Deputy Director, External Affairs
Noella Benvenuti	Deputy Director, Internal Affairs
Carol Rector	Curator, Anthropology
Robin Laska	Curatorial staff, Anthropology
Margaret Foss	Curator, Education
Holly Segni	Exhibits Designer
Robert Coutts	Exhibits staff
Nancy Fawcett	Exhibits staff
Jennifer Reynolds	Public Information Officer

ACKNOWLEDGMENTS

This exhibition and the resultant catalogue demonstrate the passion that Pamela and Benson Harer feel for Egyptian History, art and medicine. Their energy and enthusiasm have made this project possible. Dr. Amer El-Ahraf, Dr. Julius Kaplan and Dr. Russell Barber deserve credit for conceiving of the idea and securing the initial funding. Dr. Beverly Hendricks provided support and advice, generously allowing me the time to participate in this project. Art Butler, Beverly Dyer and Debbie Allen from the Foundation for CSUSB were very helpful and supportive. Cynthia Pringle and her staff provided expert help with public relations.

Dr. Gerry Scott, III, Curator of Ancient Art from The San Antonio Museum of Art, provided his expertise and artful eye to the selection of the objects, creating an exciting and cohesive exhibit. His text for the catalogue is a subtle blend of art and science. His patience and wisdom have been greatly appreciated. Dr. Nancy Thomas, Associate Curator of Ancient and Islamic Art at the Los Angeles County Museum of Art, not only wrote the insightful essay introducing the text, she provided valuable assistance with installation and transportation of objects.

The staff members of the two institutions have had to do this work in addition to their regular duties. For this I am grateful. Photographers M. Robert Markovich and Steve Hopf, Graphic Designer George McGinnis, Production Coordinator Odette C. Salvaggio, Preparator Kerry Kugelman and Editors Robin Kaplan, Julius Kaplan and Katherine P. Lintault performed under extreme pressure to produce the catalogue in record time. Don Faust of Faust Printing and Wyatt Portz of Inland Color Service prepared and printed the catalogue with incredible clarity and precision.

My thanks to those mentioned and to the countless others who contributed to the success of this project. My special thanks to Shauna, my wife, and my children Jessica and Jacob for their patience with me through this project.

Richard M. Johnston, Director, University Art Gallery

PREFACE

The Harer Family Trust collection of Egyptian antiquities ranks among the most important private collections of its sort in the United States today. It is wide-ranging within the field of Egyptology and reflects the broad tastes and interests of the two principal trustees most responsible for its formation over the past seventeen years, W. Benson Harer, Jr. M.D. and Pamela K. Harer. It has been my distinct pleasure to have known the Harers and to have witnessed the creation of this most interesting collection of Egyptian art and artifacts. I have greatly benefited from the Harers' friendship and from the numerous opportunities they have generously provided me to study the collection.

Temple, Tomb and Dwelling: Egyptian Antiquities from the Harer Family Trust Collection represents some of the collection's most important objects. Because of the size and depth of the Harer Family Trust collection, it has also been possible to mount two separate, but complementary, museum installations, one in San Bernardino, the other in Redlands. The San Bernardino County Museum presents the civilization of ancient Egypt from the vantage point of cultural anthropology. The exhibition at California State University, San Bernardino's University Art Gallery, includes complementary material, focusing principally on the visual arts in ancient Egypt. Both presentations feature important works of art. That at the University Art Gallery also emphasizes the high standard of artistry often encountered in small-scale works, particularly appropriate for the gallery's intimate exhibition space.

Each museum installation examines ancient Egyptian culture through art works and artifacts found in three of that civilization's most important architectural settings: the temple, the tomb and the dwelling. When both installations are viewed, they introduce the student and general public to the material culture of the great ancient civilization that graced the banks of the Nile for more than three thousand years.

The collection comprises material from every period of Egyptian history, from the Predynastic Period to the Coptic era, including masterpieces of Egyptian sculpture, such as the *Standard-bearing Statue of a Queen*, Cat. No. 82, and the *Bust of Sekhmet*, Cat. No. 25, striking relief sculptures, works of historical importance, and various objects that reflect daily life in ancient Egypt and the specialized articles created for the ancient Egyptian funerary cult. In addition, the Harer Family Trust collection contains a fine series of ancient Egyptian *shawabti* figures and objects that explore such themes as medicine, folk art and the role of women in ancient Egypt.

Benson and Pamela Harer have painstakingly traced many objects now in the collection to other important collections and collectors, and such objects represent a significant part of the Harer Family Trust's Egyptian antiquities. Many objects derive from an Egyptian collection assembled by Emil Brugsch of the Cairo Museum and the Egyptian Antiquities Organization during the late 19th century for Anthony J. Drexel, Jr. Mr. Drexel, in turn, donated the collection to the Drexel Institute in 1895, which sold it to the then fledgling Minneapolis Institute of Arts in 1916, when the Drexel's officers decided they should concentrate the institution's efforts on teaching rather than collecting. The Minneapolis collection subsequently increased through donations made by James Ford Bell, Edward S. Harkness and Miss Lily Place until the 1950's, when the majority of the objects were once more sold, principally through dealers and by auction. One of the most beautiful of the objects now in the Harer Family Trust collection that once was on view in Minneapolis is a rare silver statuette of the goddess Satis.

Before closing, I must record the great debt that I owe in compiling this catalogue to others who generously shared their thoughts over the years with the Harers, including Dr. Richard Fazzini, Dr. Robert S. Bianchi, and Dr. James F. Romano, each of the Brooklyn Museum; Dr. Nancy Thomas of the Los Angeles County Museum of Art; Dr. Ch. Zivie, and the late Dr. Michael A. Hoffman. Any misstatements or errors, however, remain the author's responsibility. Finally, while the brief amount of time available for the preparation of this catalogue has precluded lengthy study of many of the collection's worthy objects, it is hoped that the present publication will bring the Harer Family Trust collection before a wider audience and encourage further study and research.

Gerry D. Scott, III

NOTES TO THE CATALOGUE

The catalogue is divided into two sections reflecting the content of the two complementary installations which comprise the exhibition *Temple, Tomb and Dwelling: Egyptian Antiquities From the Harer Family Trust Collection*. Cat. Nos. 1-81 represent the objects that are to be on exhibition at the San Bernardino County Museum, while Cat. Nos. 82-154 record the objects to be displayed at the University Art Gallery of the California State University, San Bernardino. Each section is preceded by an essay which places the objects within a basic context. The internal arrangement of the catalogue entries is based on exhibition themes and, to some extent, function, rather than according to strict chronology. Hence, for example, certain objects derive originally from a temple setting (Cat. Nos. 24-35; 82-85) or relate to the ancient Egyptian funerary cult (Cat. Nos. 36-64; 142-154) and are grouped together. Since certain types of objects are to be found in both installations, the form of the catalogue entries varies to avoid repetition. Those presented in the first section of the catalogue have been given full, didactic entries; those in the second section have been given more attenuated entries which nonetheless seek to convey the most essential information about the objects.

"Cat. No." refers to entry numbers in this catalogue; entry numbers that appear in other catalogues are cited as "no." Dates assigned to specific objects and periods are approximate, and the dating sequence employed is that discussed in the catalogue's chronology section. The principal dimension for each object is given in both the metric and the English systems of measurement; additional measurements are given only in the metric system. Objects which were once part of museum collections that are now in the Harer Family Trust collection have their most recent museum accession number recorded in parenthesis following the museum identification in the provenance section of the catalogue entries, if that accession number is known.

The terms "near" and "far" are more accurate than "left" and "right" parts of the human anatomy in relief figures. For a discussion of the terms, see E. R. Russmann, "The Anatomy of an Artistic Convention...," *BES* 2 (1980), p. 57 and n.2. Hieroglyphic texts on objects have been partially translated from that portion of the inscription which might interest the general museum visitor; explanatory notes have therefore been kept to a minimum.

CHRONOLOGY

NEOLITHIC PERIOD (5500-3000 B.C.)
Naqada I, Amratian Period (4000-3500 B.C.)
Naqada II, Early Gerzean Period (3500-3300 B.C.)
Naqada III, Late Gerzean Period (3300-3100 B.C.)

EARLY DYNASTIC PERIOD
Dynasty I (3100-2890 B.C.)
Dynasty II (2890-2686 B.C.)

OLD KINGDOM
Dynasty III (2686-2613 B.C.)
Dynasty IV (2613-2494 B.C.)
Dynasty V (2494-2345 B.C.)
Dynasty VI (2345-2181 B.C.)
Dynasty VII (2181-2173 B.C.)
Dynasty VIII (2173-2160 B.C.)

FIRST INTERMEDIATE PERIOD
Dynasties IX and X (2160-2040 B.C.)
Pre-unification Dynasty XI (2133-2040 B.C.)

MIDDLE KINGDOM
Post-unification Dynasty XI (2040-1991 B.C.)
Dynasty XII (1991-1786 B.C.)
Dynasty XIII (1786-1633 B.C.)

SECOND INTERMEDIATE PERIOD
Dynasty XIV (1786-1603 B.C.)
Dynasty XV-XVI, Hyksos (1674-1558 B.C.)
Dynasty XVII, Theban (1650-1558 B.C.)

NEW KINGDOM
Dynasty XVIII, Thutmosid (1558-1303 B.C.)
Dynasty XIX, First Ramesside Dynasty (1303-1200 B.C.)
Dynasty XX, Second Ramesside Dynasty (1200-1085 B.C.)

CHRONOLOGY

THIRD INTERMEDIATE PERIOD
Dynasty XXI, Tanite 1085-945 B.C.)
Dynasties XXII-XXIII, Bubastite (945-730 B.C.)
Dynasty XXIV, Pre-Saite (730-715 B.C.)

LATE PERIOD
Dynasty XXV, Kushite (760-656 B.C.)
Dynasty XXVI, Saite (664-525 B.C.)
Dynasty XXVII, First Persian Domination (525-404 B.C.)
Dynasty XXVIII (404-398 B.C.)
Dynasty XXIX (398-378 B.C.)
Dynasty XXX (378-341 B.C.)
Dynasty XXXI, Second Persian Domination (341-330 B.C.)

CONQUEST OF ALEXANDER THE GREAT (332 B.C.)

MACEDONIAN DOMINATION (332-304 B.C.)

PTOLEMAIC PERIOD (304-30 B.C.)

ROMAN CONQUEST (30 B.C.)

N.B. While there is general agreement among Egyptologists concerning most aspects of ancient Egyptian chronology, there is still debate over many details. For example, some scholars place Dynasty XXV in the Late Period, as it appears here, while others prefer to place it in the Third Intermediate Period. Similarly, there is discussion over the proper dates of the Predynastic and Early Dynastic Periods. The chronology, provided here for the convenience of the reader is based upon those found in the *Cambridge Ancient History*; William W. Hallo and William Kelly Simpson, *The Ancient Near East: A History*, New Haven 1971; and Michael A. Hoffman, *Egypt Before the Pharaohs*, New York, 1979.

(Dates are approximate.)

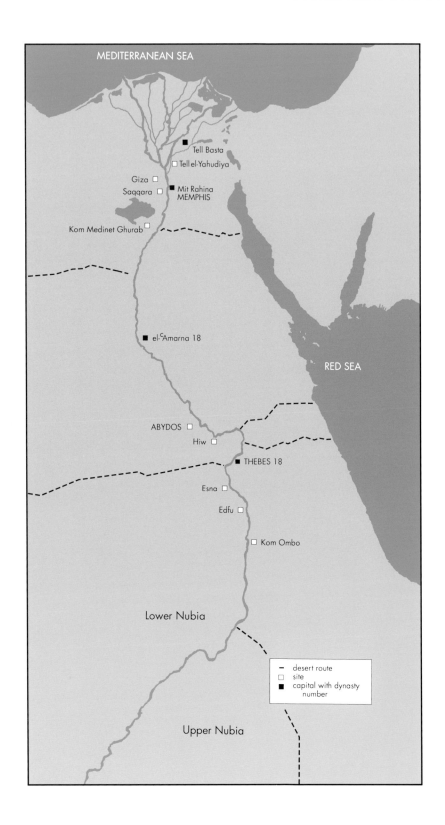

MEDITERRANEAN SEA

Tell Basta

Tell el-Yahudiya

Giza

Saqqara

Mit Rahina
MEMPHIS

Kom Medinet Ghurab

el-ʿAmarna 18

RED SEA

ABYDOS

Hiw

THEBES 18

Esna

Edfu

Kom Ombo

Lower Nubia

desert route
site
capital with dynasty
number

Upper Nubia

TEMPLE, TOMB AND DWELLING:
EGYPTIAN ANTIQUITIES FROM THE HARER FAMILY TRUST COLLECTION
Part I

INTRODUCTION

Fortuitious conditions have preserved a wide range of objects documenting the material culture of the ancient Egyptians. The combination of a dry climate and relatively isolated geography (compared to other areas of the Middle East) have allowed the survival of monumental objects in permanent materials such as limestone or basalt as well as more fragile organic materials. As a result, the depth of our knowledge about the lives of the ancient Egyptians is unrivaled by that of any other early civilization. The Harer Family Trust Collection includes over 280 objects, created in Egypt during a time period ranging from the late Predynastic era (3500 B.C.) to the mid Coptic Period (5th century A.D.). Designed for a variety of uses, the collection contains works produced by royal commission, for diverse religious purposes, or fashioned by local artisans for household consumption.

Although there is much scholarly debate concerning events leading to the establishment of the Egyptian state in approximately 3100 B. C., the archeological record clearly indicates that by this time there is a growing sophisticaton in the use of burial goods, an established pantheon of deities, and an organized political infrastructure. The period preceding this dramatic move to political unification (creating a state that remained largely intact for twenty-seven hundred years) is termed the Predynastic Period. Much of the evidence from this period is derived from the excavation of simple graves and scattered homesites in the Nile valley of Central and Upper Egypt.

The years following the political unification of Egypt are termed the Pharaonic or Dynastic period, based upon a succession of approximately thirty-one ruling families or "dynasties" of kings (pharaohs). The bulk of our knowledge concerning pharaonic Egypt is based upon evidence from royal monuments and material from the tombs of members of the upper and middle classes. The lives of these officials—the courtiers, priesthood, or wealthy landowners—who could afford elaborate sepulchres, are well documented by the reliefs, three-dimensional sculpture, and biographical and genealogical inscriptions of their tombs. In contrast, state inscriptions on temples and royal funerary monuments provide much information on the official activities of the kings, but very little is known about their daily lives.

Pharaonic history is traditionally divided into three periods of political strength and stability—the Old, Middle and New Kingdoms—separated by "Intermediate" periods of political disunity. During the so-called Late Period (760-330 B.C.), other major episodes of political intervention include a dynasty of rule by Egypt's southern neighbor (the Kushite or Nubian dynasty, 760-565 B.C.) and the Persian dominations of the 27th and 31st dynasties. The conquest of Egypt by Alexander the Great in 332 B.C. marks the final and dramatic end to Egypt's rule as an independent state. In 30 B.C., with the death of Cleopatra VIII, the Roman Empire assumes control of Egypt from the Ptolemaic kings, the heirs of Alexander. The dawn of the Christian era brings a final superimposition of non-traditional Egyptian culture to the region, as a percentage of Egypt's population adopts Christian traditions and iconography.

The theme of the two parallel exhibitions of objects from the Harer Family Collection, *Temple, Tomb and Dwelling* is based on three basic realms of ancient Egyptian existence—placed into an architectural setting—the active religious life (Temple), the Afterlife (Tomb), and aspects of everyday or domestic life (Dwelling).

Temple

The Egyptian cult temple was considered the "dwelling place of the god," and from the early Old Kingdom onward, constructed of stone and designed to be an everlasting edifice. As codified during the New Kingdom, the typical plan of the temple consisted of a two-towered pylon marking an entrance gateway and preceding a series of courts and chambers. The colossal scale and axiality of the structure focused attention on the importance of the god's shrine, an intimate and unapproachable sanctum accessible only to the king or his appointed priestly representatives. Contents of the temple, including wall scenes, ritual activities, and offerings, were intended to contribute to the god's well-being, and encourage the god (along with other deities in the pantheon) to reside within the temple. Objects in the Harer collection, such as the *Relief Depicting a Procession of Gods* (Cat. No. 26) originally adorned the wall of a temple or shrine while sculpture such as the highly important work, *Standard-Bearing Statue of a Queen* (Cat. No. 82) depicts a specific individual participating in a temple procession. Other works served as dramatic components of temple sculptural programs such as the massive *Sekhmet* (Cat. No. 25) or were dedicated by pious temple visitors (Cat. Nos. 27, 28). A large number of objects in the Harer collection may be considered in the category of votive offerings to the gods, and range from statuettes of individual deities to ex-votos offered to the gods for answered prayers.

Tomb

Fundamental to the ancient Egyptian religious view was the concept that the deceased, if deemed worthy at the time of Final Judgement, would continue life in the Netherworld and should be supplied with the accoutrements of daily life. This was accomplished both by magical means, with texts, spells, and wall scenes describing these material possessions and by the inclusion of furniture, food offerings and objects representative of the equipment of daily life in the tomb. Private burials from the Predynastic Period reveal the early onset of this practice, and the most frequent burial items include ceramic and stone vessels, cosmetic palettes for grinding pigments, and a variety of personal jewelry and amulets.

With the beginning of private tomb building in stone, during the Fourth Dynasty, wealthy private individuals were more substantially equipped for the afterlife. Remarkable wall scenes from the interior rooms of *mastaba* tombs, such as examples at Giza and Saqqara, depict scenes such as hunting in the marshes, agricultural scenes (Cat. No. 37), the slaughtering of oxen, and long processions of offering bearers with a wide range of items (Cat. No. 36). The offering chapel of these tombs provided a focal point for the mortuary cult as the deceased symbolically received sustenance from an offering table (Cat. No. 44) placed before a "false door" of the chapel. Statuary of the deceased and family were at times placed within the tomb or carved from the bedrock of the tomb walls as a means of insuring the continuing presence of the tomb owner and an additional way of allowing the deceased to receive offerings (Cat. Nos 38-42). Alternatively, an outstanding example from the Harer collection, the Kneeling Pair Statue of Senedjem (Cat. No. 45), was probably placed in an exterior location, in a niche near the top of the tomb's pyramidion. Funerary equipment likely to have been placed in tomb burial chambers include images of deities such as Osiris (Cat. No. 51) or the syncretistic god of the Late Period, Ptah Sokar-Osiris (Cat. No. 142). Also included in this category are canopic jars which held the viscera of the deceased (Cat. No. 50) and *shawabti* figures, small servant statuettes which were intended to magically serve the deceased in the afterlife. In addition to significant examples of royal shawabti (Cat. Nos. 58-61), the Harer collection contains *shawabti* of a wide range of materials and dating. Additional examples of tomb objects from the Harer collection include pieces which would have been placed on the body of the tomb owner: beads from a faience funeral shroud (Cat No. 1K), a scarab pectoral (Cat. No. 64), amulets, and three mummy masks (Cat. Nos. 49, 70, 71).

Dwelling

Much of the information about ancient Egyptian daily life is derived from tomb objects and reliefs, as illustrated by the preceding paragraphs. Objects from the Harer collection which provide information on the activities of ancient daily life include models of structures, such as the granary (Cat. No. 129), or of individuals involved in activities, such as the model of a brewer (Cat. No. 130). Actual objects which were probably derived from homes, such as the *Lamp* (Cat. No. 1Q), or the *Mortar and Pestle* (Cat. Nos. 127D, E) allow the modern viewer to more clearly visualize the domestic environment. The Harer collection contains a range of ceramic vessels designed for everyday use, as well as imported ware types (Cat. Nos. 21B, D), and more luxurious containers, such as the core-formed glass juglet (Cat. No. 20H). Cosmetic jars and implements produced in a wide range of materials, including faience, alabaster, anhydrite, or copper (Cat. Nos. 20A-E, 22), were likely to have served an elegant role in daily life, as well as burial objects for interment in the tomb. A final aspect of ancient Egyptian domestic life illuminated by the Harer collection are the objects of personal devotion, pieces which may have been placed in household shrines or worn as protective amulets (Cat. Nos. 106-115).

The Harer collection spans a time period of roughly three and a half millennia and provides a revealing view of Egyptian spiritual and domestic life.

Nancy Thomas

3

VIEW OF THE EDFU TEMPLE

Modern interest in ancient Egypt essentially dates to Napoleon Bonaparte's Egyptian campaign. Bonaparte's French troops invaded Egypt in 1798 with the aim of challenging Britain's colonial supremacy in the East. Although Napoleon's brilliant military campaign was ultimately foiled by the British navy, the large contingent of scholars, scientists, artists, and savants who accompanied his expedition succeeded in opening Egypt's past to modern scholarship. Their findings were published in the monumental *Description de l'Egypte*, consisting of ten folio volumes and two atlases illustrated with 837 copperplate engravings. This view of the temple of Edfu is typical of the intricate detail and high level of artistry found in the illustrations.

LITERATURE:

Recent publications of the Napoleonic expedition's reports include Charles C. Gillispie and Michel Dewachter, *Monuments of Egypt, The Napoleonic Edition*, Princeton, 1987, and Robert Anderson and Ibrahim Fawzy, *Egypt Revealed, Scenes from Napoleon's Description de l'Egypte*, Cairo and London, 1987.

VIEW OF THE EDFU TEMPLE
From *Description de l'Egypte*, Vol. I, pl. 49, Paris, 1809.
Drawn by Dutertre, engraved by Dutertre and Beaugean
H. of image: 40 cm. (15 3/4")
W. of image: 74 cm.

1. SELECTION OF ANTIQUITIES COLLECTED BY F. HOWLETT

The culture of ancient Egypt has long excited the imagination of visitors. Such famed classical authors as Herodotus, Diodorus, and Pliny the Elder were much impressed with the wonders of ancient Egyptian civilization and took pains to record their observations, as well as the sometimes fanciful tales told by local guides. Following the Napoleonic Wars, many Europeans and Americans visited Egypt and assembled small collections of antiquities as souvenirs of their travels. One such was an Englishman named Howlett who appears to have visited Egypt, Greece, and Italy in 1846. The various objects he collected reflect the types of antiquities then available to visitors of middle-class means, and are an interesting cultural document, both of ancient Egypt and of nineteenth-century tourism.

1. BIBLIOGRAPHY:
Christies (London) 17 November 1977, lot no. 424.

1 A. DESCRIPTION:
A series of wooden figures and parts from wooden models. Two of the three male figures are probably from the same model, while the large-scale female figure must certainly derive from a different source.

1 C. DESCRIPTION:
A fragment of border decoration from a wall of King Seti I's tomb in the Valley of the Kings at Thebes. The bands of pigment are as follows: white, black, red, black, white, black, blue (viewer's left to right). The fragment also bears a 19th century ink inscription: "Belzoni's Tomb THEBES," and an affixed paper label that states: "Fragment of painted limestone: Tomb of *Seti* (Father of Rameses is commonly called 'Belzoni's Tomb' Valley of the Kings THEBES. cir. B.C. 1400.")

1 D. DESCRIPTION:
The fragment, from a tomb inscription, preserves three fragmentary columns of hieroglyphic text; which record the tomb owner's titles and a portion of his name: "fanbearer [on the king's right hand], lord mayor, and vizier...-nakht." A handwritten label affixed to the back of the fragment, probably written by Mr. Howlett, states: "Fragment of Hieroglyphs, tomb at THEBES."

1 D. PROVENANCE:
Thebes.

1 A. FIGURES FROM MODELS

Painted wood
Middle Kingdom, Dynasty XI-XII, ca. 2040-1786 B.C.
H. of female figure: 15.8 cm. (6 3/16")

1 B. SAMPLE OF NUMMULITIC LIMESTONE

L. 9.9 cm. (3 1/2")

1 C. FRAGMENT OF WALL DECORATION

Painted limestone
Dynasty XIX, ca. 1303-1200 B.C.
L. 11 cm. (4 3/8")

1 A

1 D. INSCRIPTION FRAGMENT

Limestone
Probably late New Kingdom, ca. 1300-1000 B.C.
H. 7.3 cm. (2 7/8")

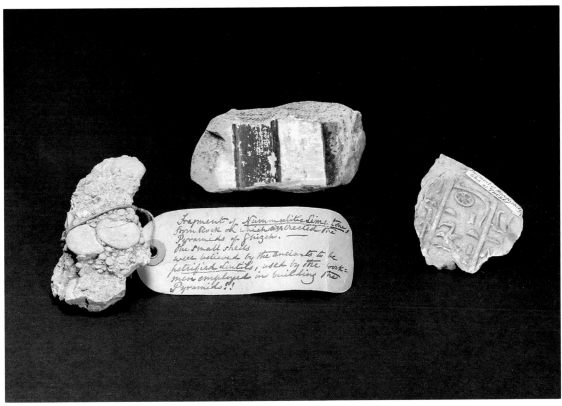

1 B, C, D

7

1 E, F, G

1 E. COMMENT:

The bust is a fragment from a sculptural jar.

1 F. DESCRIPTION:

A partially preserved votive statuette of a male god or a king wearing the *shendyt* kilt. The pleats of the kilt and details of the belt and flail are incised. The head, left shoulder, and much of the left breast are broken away and are now lacking. The surface is encrusted and shows a light green patina.

1 G. DESCRIPTION

A fragmentary figure of an ichneumon, probably from a votive coffin. The four legs and most of the tail have been broken off, and the encrusted surface shows a light green patina.

1 E DETAIL

1 E. BUST OF BES

Green-glazed faience
Late Period - Ptolemaic Period, ca. 664-30 B.C.
H. 7.4 cm. (2 7/8")

1 F. STATUETTE OF A DEITY OF KING

Bronze
Late Period - Ptolemaic Period, ca. 664-30 B.C.
H. (including tangs): 12.7 cm. (5")
H. (excluding tangs): 10 cm.

1 G. ICHNEUMON

Bronze
Late Period - Ptolemaic Period, ca. 664-30 B.C.
L. 7.6 cm. (3")

1 H. FRAGMENTARY STATUETTE OF NEFERTEM

Pale blue-glazed faience
Late Period - Ptolemaic Period, 760-30 B.C.
H. 6.5 cm. (2 5/8")

1 I. SCARAB FROM A WINGED SCARAB PECTORAL

Slate
Late Period, 760-330 B.C.
L. 6.8 cm. (2 3/4")

1 J. HEAD OF A RAM WEARING THE DOUBLE CROWN

Black steatite
Ptolemaic Period - Roman Period, ca. 300 B.C. - A.D. 100
H. 2.8 cm. (1/8")

1 H

1 I

1 J. COMMENTS:

The head, probably intended to represent either the god Amen or the god Khnum, is from a small votive statuette.

1 J

9

1 K. **"MUMMY BEAD" NECKLACES AND SAMPLES OF "MUMMY CLOTH"**
Glazed faience and linen
New Kingdom - Late Period, ca. 1500-300 B.C.
L. of necklaces: left) 26 cm. (l0 1/4")
right) 37 cm. (14 1/16")

1 L. **MINIATURE STAMP SEAL IN THE FORM OF A FROG**
Glazed faience
New Kingdom, ca. 1558-1085 B.C.
L. 0.9 cm. (3/4")

1 M. **EYE OF HORUS AMULET**
Blue-glazed faience
New Kingdom - Late Period, ca. 1500-300 B.C.
L. 2.5 cm.

1 N. **FRAGMENTARY STATUETTE OF ANUBIS**
Black serpentine
New Kingdom - Late Period, ca. 1500-300 B.C.
H. 2.5 cm. (l")

1 O. **FLORAL BEAD**
Glazed faience
New Kingdom, Dynasty XVIII-XX, ca. 1558-1085 B.C.
Diam. 1.5 cm. (5/8")

1 P. **"PILGRIM FLASK"**
Terracotta
New Kingdom, Dynasty XVIII, ca. 1558-1303 B.C.
H. 14 cm. (5 1/2")

1 Q. **LAMP WITH FISH DECORATION**
Terracotta
Ptolemaic Period - Roman Period, 2nd century B.C. - 2nd century A.D.
L. 9.5 cm. (3 3/4")

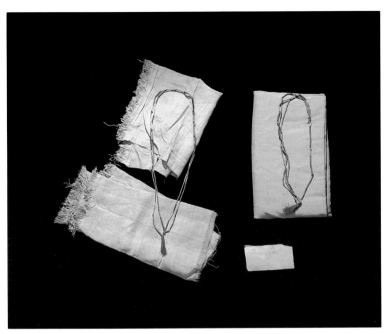

1 K

1 L

1 M

1 N

1 O

1 P, Q

11

1 S. DESCRIPTION

The figure stands on a plinth and has a narrow back pillar that rises from the plinth to the base of the wig. The facial features are well executed as are the details of the wig, beard, and hands. A hoe appears in either hand, a bag is slung over the left shoulder.

1 R. BOTTLE CONTAINING VARIOUS SAMPLE SPECIMENS FOUND IN AN EQYPTIAN TOMB
H. 14 cm. (5 1/2")

1 S. SHAWABTI FIGURE
Green-glazed faience
Late Period - Ptolemaic Period, ca. 664-30 B.C.

1 T. MINIATURE BRAZIER
Bronze
Roman, ca. 1st century B.C. - 1st century A.D. (?)
H. 12 cm. (4 3/4")

1 U. BEAD
Glazed terracotta
Probably Greek (Attic), ca. 5th - 2nd century B.C.
Diam. 1.5 cm. (5/8")

1 V. TWO ARROWHEADS
Iron
Greek, ca. 6th - 3rd century B.C.
L. O.7 cm. (11/16")

1 W. RED-FIGURE VASE FRAGMENT
Glazed terracotta
Greek (Attic), ca. 5th - 4th century B.C.
L. 4.5 cm. (1 3/4")

2. BLACK-TOPPED JARS
Terracotta
Predynastic Period (Naqada II-III), ca. 3500-3100 B.C.

Black-topped pottery formed an important class of Predynastic Egyptian ceramics. Made from river clay and given a red slip, the blackened top and interior were created by oxidizing the surface unequally during the firing process. One example here, however, has its black top added in paint (2B).

2 A-E

2 A. JAR
H. 12 cm. (4 3/4")
Diam. at lip: 7.1 cm.

2 B. TALL FLASK
H. 21 cm. (8 1/4")
Diam. at lip: 6 cm.

2 C. BOWL
H. 6.9 cm. (2 5/8")
Diam. at lip: 14.8 cm.

2 D. JAR
H. 13.4 cm. (5 1/4")
Diam. at lip: 6.5 cm.

2 E. JAR
H. 24.7 cm. (9 3/4")
Diam. at lip: 8.5 cm.

3 A. COMMENT:
This example has a potter's mark incised on its exterior.

3. BLACK-TOPPED JARS
Terracotta
Predynastic Period (Naqada II-III), ca. 3500-3100 B.C.

3 A. JAR
H. 46 cm. (18 1/8")
Diam. at lip: 24.5 cm.

3 A

3 B. JAR
H. 35.5 cm. (14")
Diam. at lip: 16.3 cm.

3 B

17

4. PREDYNASTIC POTTERY

Terracotta
Predynastic Period (Naqada II-III), ca. 3500-3100 B.C.

In addition to black-topped ware, Egyptian potters of the Predynastic Period produced several other types of ceramic vessels. Polished red ware, represented here by a bottle- shaped vase, was achieved by simple polishing of the surface with a pebble. Wavy-handled ware, first produced in Palestine but adopted by Egyptian artisans, provides an important dating criterion because the handles vary over time. The present example shows a regularly undulating handle that completely encircles the jar. The vessel is further decorated by the addition of a painted crosshatch pattern, probably intended to simulate netting. During the latter part of the Predynastic Period, squat jars were made that imitate stone vessels. The painted spirals on this example were intended to imitate the natural occlusions often found in the stone models.

4 A. LITERATURE
See Bourriau (1981), cat. no. 73, p. 74; Patch (1990), cat. no. 1b, pp. 4-5.

4 B. COMMENT:
Labeled "W4EPD" in black ink on lip.

4 B. PARALLELS:
Bourriau (1981), cat. no. 259, pp. 132- 133; Scott (1986), cat. no. 14, p. 36.

4 B. LITERATURE:
For a series of wavy-handled jars, see Hayes (1953), fig. 13, p. 11.

4 C. PARALLELS:
Bourriau (1981), cat. no. 36b, p. 29; Scott, (1986), cat. no. 8B, p. 30.

4 A, B, C

4 A. POLISHED RED FLASK

H. 16.5 cm. (6 1/2")
Diam. at lip: 5.4 cm.

4 B. WAVY-HANDLED JAR

H. 27.3 cm. (10 3/4")
Diam. at rim: 11.2 cm.

4 C. SQUAT JAR

H. 10.4 cm. (4 1/4")
W. at lug handles: 8.3 cm.

5. FISH PALETTE
Slate
Predynastic Period (Naqada II), ca. 3300 B.C.
L. 12.4 cm. (4 7/8")

5. PARALLELS:

See Lowie 6-17557 in Elsasser (1966), p. 17; Scott (1986), cat. no. 16A, p. 38; Hoffman (1988), cat. no. 64, pp. 80-81.

5. FISH PALETTE

Slate palettes are among the most common grave goods found in Predynastic burials. These palettes appear to have been intended for grinding eye paint and other cosmetic pigments, as the remains of red ocher on this example demonstrate. In addition to their utilitarian function, however, palettes also seem to have had a ceremonial use and are hence often found in funerary and religious contexts. The fish-shaped palette shown here has a notched tail and a single drilled hole at the top for suspension. Professor Michael Hoffman, who examined this example, dated it to the Naqada II Period.

6. STONE VESSELS

Vessels manufactured from a wide variety of stones were an important aspect of ancient Egyptian craftsmanship. Initiated during the Predynastic Period, the production of stone vessels continued through the Dynastic era with many of the finest examples created, like these, during the Early Dynastic Period and the succeeding Old Kingdom. Alabaster, because of its multi-colored band patterns and translucent quality, was particularly prized as a raw material for stone vessels. While such vessels were no doubt used by the privileged in life, they were also often included in burials as luxury grave goods. Occasionally stone vessels were later reused in antiquity, as is demonstrated by the Old Kingdom bowl that was later reinscribed for a Middle Kingdom priest (No. 6B).

6 A. CYLINDER JAR

Alabaster
Old Kingdom, Dynasty III, ca. 2686-2613 B.C.
H. 12.3 cm. (4 7/8")
Diam. 5.9 cm.

6 B. BOWL

Alabaster
Old Kingdom, Dynasty III, ca. 2686-2613 B.C.
H. 9.5 cm. (3 3/4")
Diam. 21.4 cm.

6 C. VASE

Alabaster
Early Dynastic Period, Dynasty II, ca. 2890-2686 B.C.
H. 8.5 cm. (3 3/8")
Diam. at rim: 4 cm.

6 A-E

6 D. JAR

Indurated limestone
Early Dynastic Period, Dynasty I-II, ca. 3100-2686 B.C.
H. 5.7 cm. (2 1/4")
Diam. at handles: 8.7 cm.
Diam. at rim: 7.7 cm.

6 E. CYLINDER JAR

Alabaster
Old Kingdom, Dynasty III-VIII, ca. 2686-2160 B.C.
H. l9cm. (7 1/2")
Diam. at rim: 13.5 cm.

6 B. DESCRIPTION:

A mottled alabaster bowl with a flat base and incurving rim. The interior of the base is very lightly marked with an incised circle.

6 B. INSCRIPTION:

"The Overseer of the *Wab*-priests of Horus, Protector-of-his-father, Senwosret-ankh, the Priest of Hemen and Priest of Horus of Nekhen."

6 B. BIBLIOGRAPHY:

Christies (London), 2 July 1982, no. 116, p. 21.

6 C. DESCRIPTION:

The vase has a flat base and a slightly raised external rim. Originally, the mouth would have been covered by a cap of thin sheet gold.

6 C. PARALLELS:

Spencer (1980), no. 236.

6 C. LITERATURE:

For stone vases that retain their original gold foil covers, see Smith (1960), fig. 8; and Saleh (1987), cat. nos. 15a-b.

6 D. DESCRIPTION:

The squat jar has a rounded base and two tubular lug handles that are pierced for suspension. A flat raised rim surrounds the mouth of the jar.

6 D. PARALLELS:

Spencer (1980), no. 209, p.4, pl.18.

6 E. BIBLIOGRAPHY:

Superior Stamp & Coin Co., Inc. *Ancient Art and Artifacts*, cat. no. 128, pp. 11-12.

7

7. RING STAND

New Kingdom - Third Intermediate Period, ca. 1558-715 B.C.
Blue-glazed faience
Diam. 9.6 cm. (3 13/16")

Ring stands were made to support round and pointed-base vessels. This example is made of glazed faience, a composition produced from pulverized quartz or quartz sand held together by an alkaline binder. Copper compounds were added to produce intense blue colors. Glazed faience was a favorite material for the ancient Egyptian craftsman and was used for a variety of decorative objects from utilitarian items such as this ring stand to amulets, jewelry, and statuettes.

7. PROVENANCE:
Ex-collections Drexel, MIA (16.485).

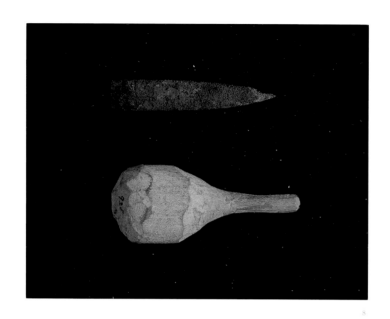

8

9

8. MALLET AND CHISEL OR ADZE

Wood and copper
New Kingdom - Late Period, ca. 1500-300 B.C.
H. of mallet: 8.9 cm. (3 1/2")
L. of chisel: 8 cm. (3 1/8")

Mallets and chisels, of various sizes, were used by ancient Egyptian artisans when carving stone or wood. The small size of this mallet may indicate that it served a votive purpose, rather a purely functional one.

8. PROVENANCE:

Ex-collections Drexel, MIA (16.515, 16.528, respectively).

8. LITERATURE:

For a full-size mallet and a stonemason's chisel found at Deir el-Bahari, see *EGA*, cat. nos. 25,26; for ancient depictions of sculptors at work, see Wilkinson (1983), p. 90 (ill. nos. 31.6.27, 31.6.10, 30.4.90).

9. DISH WITH LUMPS OF BLUE "FRIT"

Terracotta
New Kingdom - Late Period, ca. 1500-300 B.C.
L. of dish: 9 cm. (3 1/2")

Color is an important aspect of both the "fine" and "decorative" arts of ancient Egypt. Pigmented glazes enhanced objects made from faience and steatite, while polychromy was indispensible to sculpture and architecture. If any one color could be most characteristic of Egyptian decorative taste, it would almost certainly be the vibrant shade of blue represented by these lumps of "frit." So characteristic of ancient Egypt is their color to modern viewers that it is now widely known as "Egyptian blue."

9. PROVENANCE:

Ex-collections Drexel, MIA (16.163, 16.466, respectively).

9. LITERATURE:

For a selection of painter's equipment in the Cairo Museum, including a similar lump of blue frit, see Saleh (1987), cat. no. 234.

10. MODEL COLUMN CAPITAL

Columns carved in imitation of plant forms are a classic element of ancient Egyptian architectural design. The papyrus and lotus, respectively the heraldic plants of Upper and Lower Egypt, and the palm were the three most common plant forms imitated in architecture. By the Late Period, two or more plant forms were often combined to create what are termed composite columns. This example appears to be essentially an open papyriform column. The square block on the top still retains its guidelines, and it is probable that the column served as a model, although it may have ultimately had a votive function as well.

10. LITERATURE:
See Berlin (1967), cat. nos. 994-995.

11. ROYAL HEAD

Plaster was used by sculptors in ancient Egypt for nonaesthetic reasons: to hide imperfections in stone, to correct mistakes, or to conceal figures or inscriptions that were to be deleted from a composition for social or political reasons. In addition, plaster was used for experimental works, and it is possible that this head, probably once showing a king wearing the Red Crown of Lower Egypt, served as a sculptor's model. As with the papyrus column (Cat. No. 10), however, a votive or commemorative use for the head should not be ruled out.

11. PROVENANCE:
Ex-collections Place, MIA (25.222).

11. LITERATURE:
For a recent discussion of plaster heads in Egyptian art, see Brooklyn (1988), cat. no. 34, p. 129. See also Münzen und Medaillen (Basel) 27 June 1974, lot. no. 107.

10

10. MODEL COLUMN CAPITAL

Limestone
Ptolemaic Period, 330-30 B.C.
H. 14.3 cm. (5 5/8")
Max. Diam. 13 cm.

11. ROYAL HEAD

Plaster
Late Period - Ptolemaic Period, 664-30 B.C.
H. 8 cm. (3 1/8")

11

12

12. HEAD OF AN OFFICIAL

Painted limestone
New Kingdom - Dynasty XVIII-XX, ca. 1558-1085 B.C.
H. 7.9 cm. (3 1/8")

14

13. HEAD OF A CAT

Painted wood
Late Period - Ptolemaic Period, 760-30 B.C.
H. 10.1 cm. (4")

13. PROVENANCE:

Ex-collections Place, MIA (29.17.42).

13. BIBLIOGRAPHY

Sotheby's (New York) 21 May 1977, lot no. 309.

14. STATUETTE OF SEKHMET

Green-glazed faience
New Kingdom, Dynasty XVIII-XX, ca. 1558-1085 B.C.
H. 19.3 cm. (7 5/8")

12. HEAD OF AN OFFICIAL

Egyptian sculpture was usually painted, either in its entirety, as is this head, or to a limited degree where the painter colored significant details of anatomy and costume allowing the natural color of the stone to show for the rest of the composition. The present example preserves red-brown pigment for the flesh (conventional for the depiction of male figures), blue for the wig, and the eye is rendered in white and black. The head derives either from a statuette or a *shawabti* figure.

13. HEAD OF A CAT

Wood was an important medium for the ancient Egyptian sculptor. Although wood was a scarce commodity in Egypt, a surprising number of wooden objects survive. This head was once part of a statuette that showed the cat seated on its haunches. Details were added in paint, as the pigment surviving on the ear demonstrates.

14. STATUETTE OF SEKHMET

Glazed faience was particularly effective for small-scale compositions, usually produced from a mold. When larger scale works were attempted, the result could occasionally be disappointing. This statuette probably represents the lion-headed goddess Sekhmet (although several female deities could be depicted with lion heads) seated on a throne. Improperly fired, the figure leans to one side and, although a detailed work, was probably cast away as unusable in antiquity.

15. MOLD HALF

Alabaster
Ptolemaic Period - Roman Period, ca. 330 B.C. - A.D. 100
H. 10.6 cm. (4 1/8")
W. 13.1 cm.

Many small-scale objects were mass-produced by ancient Egyptian craftsmen by employing reusable molds. Copper, bronze, silver, electrum, gold, glass, faience, and terracotta could each be manipulated into a desired shape through contact with a mold, either by casting, pressing, or hammering. The mold shown here was probably intended for cold hammering a thin sheet of metal foil over the bird shape carved into the stone's surface in sunk relief. The finished product would then have been affixed to a more complex work.

15. PROVENANCE:
Ex-collections Drexel, MIA (16.505).

16. FIGURINE

Blue glass
New Kingdom, Dynasty XVIII-XX, ca. 1558-1085 B.C.
H. 2.8 cm. (1 1/8")

Glass was first produced in Egypt during Dynasty XVIII (ca. 1558-1303 B.C.), when craftsmen, patronized by the royal household, created a variety of objects including vessels, inlays, jewelry, and small figural pieces. Following the New Kingdom, however, glass production seems to have fallen off, and does not appear to have been revived until the Late Period. The figurine, perhaps a miniature figure of a deity, is difficult to identify with any degree of certainty.

17. INLAY OF A ROYAL FACE

Carnelian
New Kingdom, Dynasty XVIII, ca. 1397-1303 B.C.
H. 2.2 cm. (7/8")

This small, sophisticated work probably shows the face of a king or a male deity. The detailed carving of the facial features suggests the painstaking skill of a master craftsman. Noteworthy are two flesh folds under the chin which are typical of the period that encompassed the reign of Amenhotep III, the Amarna Period and its aftermath. The face is therefore likely to have been carved at the close of Dynasty XVIII. During this period, complex decorative compositions created with inlays of colored glass, faience, or semi-precious stones attained a degree of favor, the combination of different colored materials taking the place of painted decoration. Hence, red carnelian is appropriate for male flesh color, traditionally represented by red-brown pigment on painted surfaces.

17. LITERATURE:
For stone inlays of royal faces, see Smith (1960), ill. no. 93, p. 143; *Schimmel*, cat. no. 208; Scott (1986), cat. no. 67, p. 118.

15

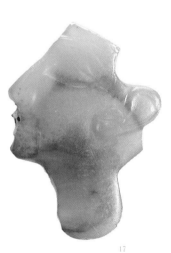

17

16

18

19

18. MATRIX FOR A MOLD

Limestone
Late Period - Ptolemaic Period, ca. 378-30 B.C.
H. 7.9 cm. (3 1/2")
L. 6.3 cm.

From the New Kingdom through the Ptolemaic Period, ancient Egyptian artists frequently enhanced their compositions, particularly in objects now associated with the decorative arts, through the use of inlays of different materials. Stone was often used, as in the previous entry (Cat. No. 17), but inlays of colored faience and glass were popular. The present object appears to be the matrix used to create a mold for producing such inlays. The facial features are crisply executed, presumably because some detail would be lost in the process of creating the terracotta mold, and again be lost when the hot glass or faience was poured into the resulting mold to create the desired inlay. Because a king or god could be shown wearing a broad array of regalia, the top of the raised relief face follows the contours of the typical base of Egyptian crowns and wigs, while the rounded neck could fit a variety of torso types. Both crown and torso could then be produced in faience or glass of differing colors from the face. The fleshy face on this matrix is perhaps reminiscent of the features of King Nectanebo II of Dynasty XXX, although some Ptolemaic rulers also display full faces.

18. BIBLIOGRAPHY:

Richard Gill, *Eternal Egypt Catalogue "Dendera"*, London, 1991, no. 14.

18. LITERATURE:

For glass and faience inlays of royalty, see Smith (1960), ill. no. 98, p. 148; Riefstahl (1968), cat. nos. 44, 76; *Schimmel*, no. 213; Matheson (1980), cat. nos. 4,6, pp. 304; Scott (1986), cat. nos. 51, 82, pp. 100, 148; Brooklyn (1989), cat. no. 87. For a wooden shrine fragment that still retains some of its inlays, see Riefstahl (1968), cat. nos. 69-71 and Brooklyn (1989), cat. no. 79. For recent studies on Egyptian glass inlays, see Robert S. Bianchi, "Those Ubiquitous Glass Inlays from Pharaonic Egypt: Suggestions about Their Functions and Date," *Journal of Glass Studies* 25 (1983), pp. 9-29; and "Those Ubiquitous Glass Inlays, Pt. II," *BES* 5 (1983), pp. 9-29.

19. COSMETIC JAR

Blue-glazed faience
New Kingdom - Third Intermediate Period, Dynasty XVIII-XXIV, ca. 1558-715 B.C.
H. 5.1 cm. (2")
Diam. at rim: 5 cm.

Throughout ancient Egyptian history, small containers for cosmetics were made from a variety of materials including precious metals, glass, faience, wood, and stone. Delicate in appearance, these intimate objects usually combine a smooth surface, an elegant shape, and a pleasing color to create an object that would well complement the luxury material they once contained.

20. COSMETIC CONTAINERS AND IMPLEMENTS

The ancient Egyptians were much concerned with personal cleanliness and appearance and seem to have indulged this interest in accordance with their means. Luxury goods associated with grooming took many different forms and were fashioned from a range of materials that included stone, wood, glass, faience, and metal. Particularly noteworthy in the present selection is the anhydrite container, dating to the Middle Kingdom, with its sealed top intact. Powdered cosmetics stored in either single vessels or multi-chambered containers would typically be placed on a mixing palette by means of a metal or wooden spoon or applicator where they would be joined with a liquid and then applied to the body.

20 A. KOHL JAR WITH LID
Alabaster
New Kingdom, Dynasty XVIII, ca. 1558-1303 B.C.
H. at rim: 7.6 cm. (3")
Diam. at rim: 6.8 cm.
Diam. of lid: 6.8 cm.

20 B. COSMETIC JAR
Anhydrite
Middle Kingdom, Dynasty XI-XIII, ca. 2040-1633 B.C.
H. 5.4 cm. (2 1/8")

20 C. COSMETIC VESSEL
Blue-glazed faience
New Kingdom - Late Period, ca. 1558-330 B.C.
H. 3.4 cm. (1 1/4")
Diam. at rim: 3.9 cm.

20 D. COSMETIC JAR
Blue-glazed steatite
New Kingdom - Late Period, ca. 1558-330 B.C.
H. 3.6 cm. (1 1/2")
Diam. at rim: 1.9 cm.

20 E. MULTICHAMBERED COSMETIC CONTAINER
Green-glazed faience
Late Period, Dynasty XXX, 378-341 B.C.
L. 8.5 cm. (3 3/8")
W. 9.2 cm.

20 F. PALETTE
Slate
Late Period, Dynasty XXV-XXXI, ca. 760-330 B.C.
L. 10.2 cm. (4")
W. 6.9 cm.

20 A-I

20 G. COSMETIC SPOON

Bronze
Late Period, Dynasty XXV-XXXI, ca. 760-330 B.C.
L. 5.6 cm. (2 1/4")

20 H. JUG

Glass
Late Period, Dynasty XXVI-XXXI, ca. 664-330 B.C.
H. 6.7 cm. (2 3/4")

20 I. JUGLET (TELL EL-YAHUDIYA WARE)

Terracotta
Second Intermediate Period, ca. 1650-1558 B.C.
H. 5.9 cm. (2 5/16")
Diam. at lip: 2.5 cm.

20 A. PROVENANCE:

Ex-collections Robert Hay, C. Granville Way, BMFA (72.531).

20 A. BIBLIOGRAPHY:

Sotheby's (New York) 18 June 1991, lot no. 9.

20 A. PARALLELS:

See Patch (1990), cat. no. 42e, pp. 56-57.

20 B. BIBLIOGRAPHY:

Malter & Co. (Los Angeles) 26 February 1978, lot no. 210.

20 D. PROVENANCE:

Ex-collections Drexel, MIA (16.259).

20 E. PROVENANCE:

Ex-collections Place, MIA. (29.17.27).

20 E. DESCRIPTION:

Only the lower half of this three- chambered cosmetic container survives. It is made in the form of a lotus blossom, and has a hole at its base for the missing lid's pivot.

20 E. PARALLELS:

BM 63980; Louvre E.11045 in Vandier d'Abbadie (1972), no. 132, pp. 47-48; Richmond 55-8-12 in Virginia (1973), cat. no. 39.

20 F. DESCRIPTION:

The palette is roughly oval in shape with a recessed central depression and channel. Traces of blue pigment remain in the hollowed area.

20 G. PARALLELS:

See Petrie (1927/1974), no. 56, p. 28, pl XXIII; Vandier d'Abbadie (1972), no. 52, pp. 26-27.

20 G. PROVENANCE:
Ex-collections Place, MIA (27.41.23).

20 H. DESCRIPTION:
A sandcore jug with trefoil mouth and handle. The body, handle, and foot of the glass vessel are dark blue, with characteristic two-color zigzag decoration in light blue and yellow, and a light blue thread around the lip. The shape is reminiscent of Greek pottery forms of the seventh century B.C., and this example, though possibly made in Egypt, may also be of non-Egyptian manufacture.

20 H. PARALLELS:
See Matheson (1980), cat. nos. 7, 9.

20 I. PROVENANCE:
Ex-collections Drexel, MIA (16.560).

20 I. LITERATURE:
See Bourriau (1981), pp. 41-43, 273 (cat. no. 273).

21. VESSELS

Clay vessels were used throughout ancient Egyptian history, not only for storing luxury goods, but also for storing, preparing, and serving food. In addition, ceramics manufactured in other parts of the ancient Mediterranean entered Egypt along with the trade goods they contained. The present selection of New Kingdom vessels includes two Egyptian jugs with handles, a tall and narrow polished bottle of Syrian manufacture, a juglet from Cyprus, and two sherds that are representative of the highly decorative pottery produced in Egypt during the reign of Amenhotep III and the succeeding Amarna Period.

21 A. PROVENANCE:
Ex-collections Drexel, MIA (16.591).

21 A. DESCRIPTION:
A single-handled pitcher decorated in a stylized foliage motif in red-brown pigment.

21 A. PARALLELS:
See Bourriau (1981), cat. no. 150, pp. 78-79; Patch (1990), cat. no. 27a, p. 42; EGA, cat. no. 55, p. 79.

21 A. PITCHER

H. 12.4 cm. (4 7/8")
Diam. at lip: 7 cm.

21 B. RED LUSTROUS SPINDLE BOTTLE

H. 33.3 cm. (13 1/8")
Diam. at base: 3.9 cm.

21 C. AMPHORA

H. 14 cm. (5 1/2")
Diam. at lip: 7.7 cm.

21 D. BASE-RING WARE JUGLET

H.11.4 cm. (4 1/2")
Diam. at lip: 3 cm.

21 E. SHERD FROM A JAR

H. 8.6 cm. (3 3/5")
W. 6.6 cm.

21 F. SHERD FROM A JAR

H. 8.7 cm. (3 1/2")
W. 12.1 cm.

21 B. PROVENANCE:

Ex-collections Drexel, MIA (16.589).

21 B. LITERATURE AND PARALLELS:

See Bourriau (1981), cat. nos. 256a-b, pp. 129-130; Patch (1990), cat. no. 34c, p. 49; EGA, cat. no. 66, p. 85.

21 C. PROVENANCE:

Ex-collections Drexel, MIA (16.605).

21 C. PARALLEL:

Ede (1983), p. 45, no. 124.

21 D. LITERATURE AND PARALLELS:

See Bourriau (1981), cat. no. 250, p. 126; Patch (1990), cat. no. 34d.

21 E. LITERATURE:

For a complete jar of this ware, see EGA, cat. no. 73, p. 93.

21 A-F

21. VESSELS

Terracotta
New Kingdom, Dynasty XVIII, ca. 1558-1303 B.C.

22. MIRROR

Copper
Probably Middle Kingdom, Dynasty XI-XIII, ca. 2040-1633 B.C.
H. 12.7 cm. (5")
Max. Diam. of Disk: 8.3 cm.

Mirrors, made of highly polished copper or bronze to cast a good reflection, were common possessions of ancient Egypt's upper classes. The disk shape of the reflecting surface was reminiscent of the sun's disk to the ancient Egyptians, hence their mirrors are often enhanced by symbolic decoration. In this example, a pair of celestial falcons, sacred to the sun god, appropriately flank the mirror's disk. At the base of the disk appears the head of the goddess Hathor, a deity associated with beauty, vitality, and generation.

22. PROVENANCE:

Ex-collections Place, MIA (29.17.515).

22. PARALLELS:

BM 2731. For early New Kingdom mirrors with falcon decoration, see Hayes (1959), fig. 32, p. 63; *EGA*, cat. no. 214, pp. 185-186.

23. JEWELRY

Jewelry was widely worn in Egypt as early as the Predynastic Period. Necklaces, earrings, and finger rings were each popular accoutrements for daily and formal attire. Both men and women wore jewelry in ancient Egypt, and skillful craftsmen fashioned elegant creations in keeping with each patron's means.

23 A. PARALLEL:

EGA, cat. nos. 346a-d, p. 249.

23 B. PROVENANCE:

Ex-collections Drexel, MIA (16.285).

23 B. BIBLIOGRAPHY:

Sotheby's (New York) 21 May 1977, lot no. 275.

23 C. PROVENANCE:

Ex-collections Drexel, MIA (16.327).

23 C. PARALLEL:

See Cat. No. 22D, below.

23 C. LITERATURE:

See Sir W.M.F. Petrie, (1927/1974) *Objects of Daily Use*, London 1927, reissued Warminster, 1974), p. 22 (incorrectly identified as hair rings), pl. XVII, nos. 1-36; Hayes (1959), fig. 102, p. 185; *EGA*, pp. 227-228.

23 D. PROVENANCE:

Ex-collections Drexel, MIA (16.328).

23 D. PARALLEL:

See Cat. No. 23C, above.

23 A. FINGER RING WITH EYE OF HORUS

Blue-glazed faience
New Kingdom, Dynasty XVIII-XX, ca. 1558-1085 B.C.
Diam. 2.2 cm. (1 7/8")

23 B. FINGER RING WITH AEGIS OF SEKHMET

Blue-glazed faience
Third Intermediate Period, Dynasty XXI-XXIV, ca. 1085-730 B.C.
Diam. of ring: 2.3 cm. (7/8")

23 C. PENANNULAR EARRING

Red Jasper
New Kingdom, Dynasty XVIII-XX, ca. 1558-1085 B.C.
Diam: 1.7 cm. (11/16")

23 D. PENANNULAR EARRING

Red Jasper
New Kingdom, Dynasty XVIII-XX, ca. 1558-1085 B.C.
Diam: 1.7 cm. (11/16")

23 E. NECKLACE

Carnelian
Middle Kingdom - New Kingdom, ca. 2000-1000 B.C.
L. 47.6 cm. (18 3/4")

23 F. NECKLACE

Blue-glazed faience
Third Intermediate Period, Dynasty XXI-XXIV, ca. 1085-730 B.C.
L. 31.1 cm. (12 1/4")

23 G. NECKLACE

Blue and green-glazed faience
New Kingdom, Dynasty XVIII-XIX, ca. 1558-1200 B.C.
L. 47.6 cm. (18 3/4")

23 H. NECKLACE

Glazed faience and gold
Roman Period, 1st century B.C. - 1st century A.D.
L. 59.7 cm. (23 1/2")

23 I. NECKLACE

Blue glass "tear-drop" beads and spacers of various materials
Various periods
L. 62.9 cm. (24 3/4")

23 A-D

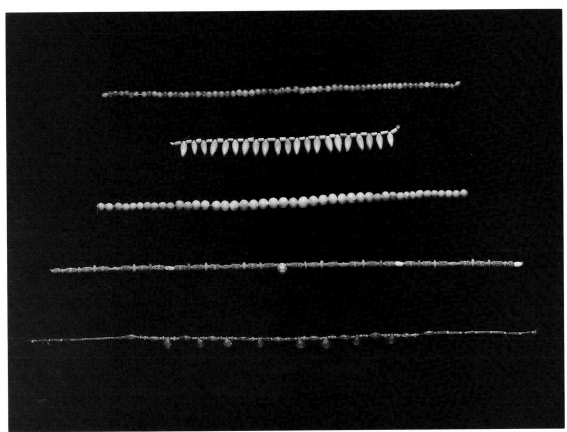

23 E-I

43

24 A

24 B

24 C

24. FRAGMENTARY BUST

Schist
Late Period, Dynasty XXVI-XXX, 664-341 B.C.
H. 15.3 cm. (6")
L. of break at neck: 10.8 cm.
L. of break at waist: 12.4 cm.

An elegant example of the masterful carving achieved by Egyptian sculptors during the Late Period, this fragmentary bust comes from a seated statue that probably depicted the god Osiris. The figure is cloaked in the close-fitting, shroud-like garment typically worn by this deity from which only the hands, throat, and head emerge. The figure's hands tightly grasp the symbols of his divine kingship, the crook and flail. Throughout, detail is carefully carved into the stone's highly polished surface. Painstakingly shown are the tiers and pendant beads of the broad collar, the details of the flail, and the thumb nails. Noteworthy is the indication of a decorated border where the hands emerge from the garment (shown by two incised lines at each wrist) and the peaked shoulder of the stiff, enveloping garment. The latter detail is more often seen in bronze figures of Osiris than in representations in stone. Also interesting is the shorter length of the now-missing divine beard, which must have terminated just at the break line at the neck. While it is tempting to link this sculpture to the famous Osiris in the Cairo Museum (CG 38358), dated to Dynasty XXVI - indeed, the Cairo example gives a fair idea of what this fragment's original appearance must surely have been - the fragmentary bust's details and its gem-like carving may also argue for a date in Dynasty XXX.

24. LITERATURE:

For a recent publication of CG 38358, see Saleh (1987), cat. no. 252.

25. BUST OF THE GODDESS SEKHMET

Gray granite
New Kingdom, Dynasty XVIII, reign of Amenhotep III,
ca. 1403-1365 B.C.
H. 99 cm. (39")

This is one of the finest examples of ancient Egyptian art in the Harer Family Trust collection. "Sekhmet," which means literally 'The Powerful One,' was typically portrayed, as here, by a head of a lioness on the body of a woman. Sekhmet was believed to embody the potentially devastating power of the blazing sun, and as such she could destroy the enemies of both the sun god and the king. Wife of the god Ptah, whose principal cult center was ancient Memphis, Sekhmet became associated with the goddess Mut, consort of the state god Amen. During the course of the New Kingdom, more than seven hundred statues of Sekhmet were placed in the temple of the goddess Mut at Karnak, the majority of them carved during the reign of Amenhotep III.

Probably part of a seated statue originally, only the head, torso, right upper arm, and a portion of a divine sun disk crown are preserved. The goddess wears a meticulously carved broad collar and the traditional sheath dress, the shoulder straps of which are decorated with a rosette at each breast. The compellingly powerful carving of the lioness face is enhanced by the subtle detail displayed in the repetitive geometric pattern lines which mark the inner ear, the mane, and the strands of the wig.

25. PROVENANCE:

Karnak, probably from the Mut Temple.

25. LITERATURE:

Münzen und Medaillen 59 (16 June 1981), lot 22, pp. 11-12, pls. 7-8.

25. PARALLELS:

Several Sekhmet statues are in American collections, including Lowie 5-365, see Fazzini (1975), cat. no. 56, pp. 76, 136 and Elsasser (1966), p. 74; for an example in the BMFA, see Smith (1960), fig. 81. For a description of two examples in Luxor, one with sun disk and one without, see Luxor (1979), cat. nos. 110-111, p. 85.

25

47

26

26. RELIEF DEPICTING A PROCESSION OF GODS
Sandstone
Ptolemaic Period, 304-30 B.C.
H. 45 cm. (17 3/4")
L. 140 cm.

A procession of twelve deities is partially preserved on this block, which once decorated the wall of a temple or shrine. It was worked in sunk relief, a technique in which the desired image is carved below the surface of the stone.

Hapi, god of the Nile, heads this procession. His full, rounded stomach complements the tray of offerings he holds before him, while a fragmentary column of hieroglyphic text behind him still records his name. Upon his head, Hapi wears his usual crown of lotus and papyrus plants, symbolizing Upper and Lower Egypt and the river Nile. Hapi also wears his traditional loin cloth of archaic form, an arm band, and a bracelet. Next is an ithyphalic image of the fertility god Min, who wears a crown decorated with twin falcon feathers and a sun disk. He balances a flail suspended aloft by his upraised hand. Interestingly, the sculptor has represented Min as a statue, indicated by the plinth, or base, on which the statue stands and by the back pillar rising from the base to the crown. The remaining deities in the procession each hold a divine *was* scepter in the far hand and an *ankh* in the near hand. Each god also wears a knee-length kilt, from the belt of which descends a divine tail, and a broad collar. The deities include a falcon-headed god, two human-headed gods wearing crowns (the second of whom is probably Onuris), a ram-headed god, a pair of gods shown in echelon fashion (one of which is probably Khepri, judging from the scarab in the sun disk above the pair), three gods also shown in echelon, and a divinity that is only partly preserved.

The technique of carving echeloned images to indicate two or three figures walking side by side is noteworthy in this relief sculpture. For the pair of gods, only a second profile face carved next to the full figure indicates the presence of another deity; while for the threesome, profile arms, legs, and feet have been carved as well. Despite the fact that the remains of vertical columns of hieroglyphs appear above and before the figures, the texts are quite fragmentary.

26. PROVENANCE:
Probably Upper Egypt.

26. PARALLELS:
Sotheby's, New York (18 June 1991), lot 53a.

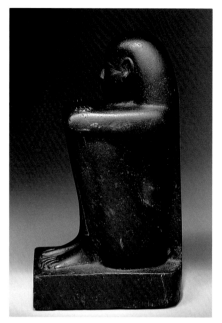

27

27. BLOCK STATUE OF WAH-IB-RE, PRIEST OF AMEN
AT KARNAK
Black basalt
Ptolemaic Period, 304-30 B.C.
H. 34 cm. (l3 3/8")

27

5
1

27. BLOCK STATUE OF WAH-IB-RE, PRIEST OF AMEN AT KARNAK

Block statues, so termed because of their compact, cubic form, mainly were employed by the ancient Egyptians as temple, or votive, statues. First introduced into the corpus of Egyptian sculptural types during the Middle Kingdom, they remained a popular form for private sculpture until the close of the Ptolemaic Period. Such statues typically represent the owner wearing a long, full cloak and a shoulder-length wig while seated on the ground with the knees drawn up toward the chest and the arms folded over the knees. This pose reduces the body to a simple cubic mass from which only the head, hands, and feet emerge. The resulting sculptural form was particularly appropriate for a private statue intended to represent its owner in eternal vigil within the temple precinct of his god. The compact form minimized the risk of breakage, and the front, back, and sides of the statue provided large, flat areas suitable for inscriptions and relief carvings. Wah-ib-re's statue is decorated only on its front surface. The priest is shown with his arms raised in adoration before the mummiform god Osiris. Both deity and worshipper are carved in sunk relief, and both are identified by the vertical hieroglyphic text columns surrounding their figures. Above, the stylized vault of heaven is indicated by a series of five-pointed stars within an elongated hieroglyph meaning "sky." Interestingly this combination of three-dimensional statue with two-dimensional relief representation tends to unite in one composition the functions of votive statue and votive stela.

27. PROVENANCE:

Karnak, Temple of Amen, Cachette.

27. BIBLIOGRAPHY:

Galerie Georges Petit, Paris (25 May 1914), lot 4, p. 8. PM Vol. II, pt. 2, p. 165.
Sotheby's, London (13 December 1977), lot 192 and pl. XXXVI.
Superior (1978), Cat. No. 3, p. 10.
R.A. Fazzini in Brooklyn Museum, (1988), cat. no. 29, pp. 123-124.

28. STRIDING STATUE OF THE PRIEST IMHOTEP

The striding statue of Imhotep depicts him wearing a long, high-waisted kilt that extends from a point just below the breasts to the ankles. It folds right side over left, and its opening is indicated by an incised line. He grasps a staff with a floral finial in his left hand as well as a folded cloth. On either side of his garment is a sunk relief figure of a female relative. On Imhotep's left is his mother, Isis-weret, and on his right is the sunk relief image of his daughter, who is also named Isis-weret. Each figure raises one hand and is identified by a single, vertical column of hieroglyphic text before her. The costumes, however, differ. Imhotep's mother wears a more traditional sheath dress and simple, traditional wig. His daughter wears a full, fringed gown of the type popularly depicted during the Ptolemaic Period and a more fashionable wig. This use of different costumes to distinguish age or generational distinctions reflects a long-standing artistic tradition also found in the pair statue Senedjem (Cat. No. 45).

Imhotep is similarly identified by a single, vertical column of hieroglyphic text incised on the front of his kilt and another on the back pillar. The inscriptions record his priestly titles in the service of the gods Amen and Thoth, as well as recording the name of his father, Horsiese (?) and his mother Isis-weret.

28. BIBLIOGRAPHY:

Sotheby's (London) 8 December 1980, lot no. 126.

28. NB.

The height given above is the preserved height of the ancient sculpture, from the break at the neck to the ankles. The statue base and feet, though possibly ancient, did not belong to this sculpture in antiquity.

28 DETAIL

28

28 DETAIL OF BACK

28

28. STRIDING STATUE OF THE PRIEST IMHOTEP

Limestone
Ptolemaic Period, 304-30 B.C.
H. 34.2 cm. (13 1/2")

5
5

29 A

30

29 B

29. SITULAS
Bronze
Ptolemaic Period, 304-30 B.C.

Situlas are ceremonial vessels that contained a liquid, usually water, used in religious rituals and funerary rites. These two examples are cast bronze and are decorated with registers of raised relief. In each case, the central register depicts a series of striding deities. The rounded base of both vessels is decorated with a lotus motif.

29 A. SITULA
H. (excluding handle): 19.3 cm. (7 5/8")

29 B. SITULA
H. (excluding handle): 13 cm. (5 1/8")

29 B. PROVENANCE:
Ex-collections Drexel, MIA (16.45).

30. STATUETTE OF A PRIEST
Bronze
Late Period, Dynasty XXV-XXX, 760-341 B.C.
H. 7.3 cm. (2 7/8")

This small statuette of a worshipping priest is interesting in its detail. The figure kneels with the buttocks resting on the backs of the ankles, and with hands raised in adoration. A back pillar runs from the back of the priest's head to a point just above his feet, and the tenoned rectangular base suggests that he was once part of a larger composition. An image of the god Osiris, probably the deity receiving the priest's attention, rests in his lap. It is also supported by a suspension cord that passes diagonally over the priest's left shoulder. The priest wears a close-fitting cap, a pleated *shendyt* kilt, and arm bands. These details of costume perhaps argue for an early date in the Late Period for this statuette.

30. BIBLIOGRAPHY:
Carnegie Institute, *Ancient Bronzes, A Selection from the Heckett Collection*, Pittsburg, 1964, Cat. No. 40.
Sotheby's (New York) 21 May 1977, lot no. 352.

31. STATUETTES OF OSIRIS, ISIS AND HORUS
Bronze
Late Period, Dynasty XXVI-Ptolemaic Period, 664-30 B.C.

The ancient Egyptians worshipped a number of deities, many of whom were primarily of regional importance. However, the resurrected god of the dead, Osiris, together with his wife Isis, and son Horus, received veneration throughout the land. Usually depicted as a mummiform king, Osiris was worshipped as a guarantor of the afterlife. His consort Isis personified the devoted wife and mother, as well as the effective magician, whose spells raised Osiris from death and ensured the survival of his royal offspring Horus.

31 A. DESCRIPTION:
The goddess is shown in the usual manner: seated as she suckles her infant son. She wears a traditional wig, a sheath dress, and a crown consisting of horns, disk, and uraeus serpents.

31 B. DESCRIPTION:
Osiris is depicted as mummiform and wearing a white crown decorated with two plumes and the uraeus serpent. He also wears a divine beard and holds the traditional crook and flail in fisted hands that emerge from the mummy cloth. There are traces of inlay at the eyes and gilding on the body.

31 B. PARALLEL:
Richmond 55-32-2, see Virginia (1973), cat. no. 59, p. 52.

32. FIGURES OF DEITIES

The ancient Egyptian pantheon consisted of several gods, some of national significance, others of mainly local importance. During the later periods of ancient Egyptian history, small statuettes of these gods were made in both bronze and faience to be used as votive gifts. Purchased by the devout, these miniature cult images were then offered to the deity as a token of personal devotion, in thanksgiving, or as an element of petition. Statuettes of three deities are represented: Neith, a goddess of the Delta whom the Greeks identified with Artemis; Ptah, the creator god of the ancient city of Memphis; and the cat-headed goddess Bast.

32 C. BIBLIOGRAPHY:
Ede (1983), p. 94, no. 246.

31 A. ISIS AND HORUS
H. 16.9 cm. (6 5/8")

31 B. OSIRIS
H. 13.2 cm. (5 1/2")

31 A, B

32 A

32. FIGURES OF DEITIES
Bronze
Late Period - Ptolemaic Period, 760-30 B.C.

32 B

32 C

32 A. PTAH
H. 11.4 cm. (4 1/2")

32 B. NEITH
H. 24.2 cm. (9 5/8")

32 C. BAST
H. 15.8 cm. (6 1/4")

33 A, B

33 A. AEGIS
Bronze
H. 9.8 cm. (3 15/16")

33 B. AEGIS
Glazed faience
H. 7 cm. (2 3/4")

33. THE AEGIS
Late Period - Ptolemaic Period, 760-30 B.C.

The Greek term 'aegis' describes an ancient Egyptian device with protective and amuletic properties. The Egyptian aegis typically consists of the head of an important deity surmounting a broad collar. Of different materials, both examples in the Harer Family Trust collection show the head of ram-headed Amen crowned with sundisk and uraeus serpent. Interestingly, the bronze statuette of the goddess Bast (Cat. No. 32C) holds a similar aegis in the left hand.

33 A. PARALLEL:
Ede (1983), p. 94, no. 251.

34. STATUETTES OF ANIMALS
Bronze
Late Period - Ptolemaic Period, 760-30 B.C.

Animal depictions were among the most appealing art objects made in ancient Egypt. They were central to the cults of many of Egypt's gods, and images of these animals were made in great numbers to function as either votive gifts or as amulets. The bronze statuettes in the Harer Family Trust collection demonstrate the ancient Egyptian artist's ability to capture the essence of a particular species. The cat was especially associated with the goddess Bast (Cat. No. 32C), while the ichneumon, or mongoose, was associated with various deities including the god Horus, the goddess Wadjet, and the sun-god Re, who, according to tradition had transformed himself into a mongoose to defeat Apophis, evil serpent of the Netherworld. Often these bronze animals decorated a small coffin of an embalmed body of a sacred animal that had been reared at the patron deity's temple or shrine. Embalming the bodies of cult animals was believed to be pleasing to the gods, and such coffins were offered as votive gifts by the pious.

34 A. LITERATURE:
Christies (London) 31 May 1979, lot no. 166.

34 B. BIBLIOGRAPHY:
Sotheby's (New York) 12 May 1979, lot. no. 237.

34 B. PARALLEL:
Ede (1983), p. 94, no. 251.

34 C. BIBLIOGRAPHY:
Sotheby's (New York) 12 May 1979, lot. no. 242.

34 D. PROVENANCE:
Ex-collection Troy Public Library, Troy, New York.

34 D. BIBLIOGRAPHY:
Superior Stamp & Coin, *Superior Antiquities*, Los Angeles, 1974, no. 45.

34 D. LITERATURE:
For the ichneumen, see John D. Cooney, "Pharaoh's Rat," *Bulletin of the Cleveland Museum of Art*, Vol. LII, no. 8 (October, 1965), pp. 100-105. See also, *Mummies*, cat. no. 194, pp. 235-236.

34 A. CAT
H. 14 cm. (5 1/2")

34 B. FISH
L. 13.1 cm. (5 1/8")

34 C. LION-HEADED SERPENT
L. 7.9 cm. (3 1/8")

34 D. ICHNEUMON
L. 9.5 cm. (3 3/4")

34 A

34 B-D

35. VOTIVE COFFIN OF AN ICHNEUMON
Polychromed and gilded gesso on wood
Ptolemaic Period, 332-30 B.C.
H. 5.4 cm. (12 1/8")
L. 12.1 cm. (4 3/4")

35. VOTIVE COFFIN OF AN ICHNEUMON

This colorful votive coffin, once deposited in a temple or shrine as an offering, still contains the embalmed body of an ichneumon (See Cat. No. 34D). In its bright color and gilding it is typical of such votive gifts of the Ptolemaic Period. Of special interest is the dicing pattern decorating the coffin's sides.

36. OFFERING BEARERS

Relief carvings were an integral part of important Old Kingdom tombs, and the depiction of offering bearers constituted a prime motif. Such compositions show processions of male and female servants bringing the agricultural, manufactured, and natural bounty of the earth into the presence of their deceased master. These scenes continued beyond the Old Kingdom and were found in decorated tombs of the Ptolemaic Period. Three male offering bearers are partially preserved on this fragment from the tomb of an unknown Old Kingdom official. The raised relief figures were probably once part of a larger procession. Each man wears a short wig and a knee-length kilt. The first figure is heavily laden with jars suspended from cords nestled in the crook of both arms. On his near shoulder, he carries a box-like coop containing three birds, perhaps intended as pigeons. His now-missing far hand probably once balanced a tray heaped with offerings. The second figure in line carries a jar that is similarly suspended from the crook of his far arm, and he cradles a large bag or box against his chest. The very fragmentary third figure brings a waterfowl as one of his offerings. The workmanship of the relief fragment is not exceptional, yet the object displays a level of care in the treatment of detail typical for competent work of the Fifth and Sixth Dynasties.

37. RELIEF FRAGMENT FROM AN AGRICULTURAL SCENE

This interesting relief fragment with some original color was once part of a larger composition showing the measuring, winnowing, heaping, and threshing of grain. Relief depictions of agricultural activities formed a significant portion of the decorative scheme for the walls of Old Kingdom private tombs. It was thought that, through the depiction of such pursuits on tomb walls, the spirit of the deceased owner would be eternally ensured access to the foodstuffs shown. The Harer Family Trust example partially preserves three figures, that furthest to the viewer's left represented only by a section of his arm. He was once shown standing upon a heap of grain, helping to secure it in place. The central figure holds a three-tined pitch fork. His body is turned away from the heap of grain, but he swivels his head back to view it. As typical for such scenes, this worker has a stubble beard, and is thus characterized as a fieldhand. His fellows are usually clean-shaven, as is the laborer to the viewer's right. This worker, part of the threshing sequence, faces away from the heaped grain, and drives a group of now-missing asses with the stick in his upraised hands. As is often the case, he has belted up his short kilt to allow free play to his legs.

36. OFFERING BEARERS

Limestone
Old Kingdom, Dynasty V-VI, ca. 2494-2181 B.C.
H. 25.9 cm. (10")
L. 35.9 cm.

37. RELIEF FRAGMENT FROM AN AGRICULTURAL SCENE

Limestone
Old Kingdom, Dynasty V-VI, ca. 2494-2181 B.C.
H. 25.8 cm. (10 3/16")
L. 26 cm.

37

37. PRESERVED COLOR

Some red-brown pigment is preserved on the flesh of the three figures; black is preserved on the hair and stubble beard.

37. LITERATURE:

For similar scenes, see H. Wild, *Le Tombeau de Ti.*, fasc. III, pt. 2, Cairo, 1966, pl. CLV; William Kelly Simpson, *The Offering Chapel of Sekhem-ankh-ptah in the Museum of Fine Arts, Boston*, Boston (1976), pp. 15-16, fig. 9, pl. D.

38

38. STATUE OF A YOUNG GIRL (HETEP-HERES)

Limestone
Old Kingdom, Dynasty V, ca. 2494-2345 B.C.
H. 54 cm. (21 1/4")

Hetep-heres is one element of a large group statue comprised of five figures. The base of this statue was discovered by Selim Hassan in Re-wer's Giza tomb during excavations he conducted in 1929-1930. When complete, the original statue represented the tomb owner, Re-wer; his mother, Hetep-heres; his father, Ity-su; his son, also named Re-wer; and his daughter, also named Hetep- heres, who is represented by this sculpture. The group statue of Re-wer's family depicted each figure on a nearly life-size scale, and Hetep-heres is shown as a young girl, nude and with her now-missing right hand held to her mouth. This was the usual method of representing children, whether male or female (see Cat. Nos. 91, 92, 107), and a similar pose was used by the ancient Egyptians in the hieroglyphic writing for the word child (*hrd*). In addition to the statue of Hetep-heres in the Harer Family Trust collection, the present location of three other torsos from the original group sculpture is known. That of Re-wer is now in Kansas City, his father's sculpture is in Brooklyn, and his mother's sculpture is in Worcester, Massachusetts. The group statue was probably carved early in the Fifth Dynasty, and John D. Cooney tentatively assigned the work to the reign of Nefer-ir-ka-re, third king of that dynasty. The Harer sculpture of Hetep-heres is in poor condition. This head has been reattached to the body in modern times, and the face is much restored.

38. LITERATURE:

Selim Hassan, *Excavations at Giza, 1929-1930*, Oxford, 1932, pp. 27,29, pl. XXX, no.1; John D. Cooney, "A Tentative Identification of Three Old Kingdom Sculptures," *JEA* 31 (1945), pp. 54-56. The other known sculptures from the group are Kansas City 38.11, Brooklyn 37.365, Worcester 1934.48, see Vandier (1958), pl. XVII.

38. PROVENANCE:

Giza, Tomb of Re-wer.

39. FUNERARY RELIEF

Limestone
Late Old Kingdom, probably Dynasty VII-VIII, ca. 2181-2160 B.C.
H. 32.7 cm. (13")
L. 60.8 cm.

The fragment, part of a larger block from an official's tomb, was possibly a false door architrave. The carving style is typical of relief work at the close of the Old Kingdom and the beginning of the First Intermediate Period, a time when the central authority of the ancient Egyptian state collapsed. The human figures are remarkably slender, characteristic of a regional or "folk" style, executed in imitation of the earlier court style of the Old Kingdom. Similarly, some of the hieroglyphs in the text display a degree of freedom in their relative proportions.

In the main, however, the text follows time-honored tradition, and its two horizontal registers may be translated:

1. "An offering which the king gives to Anubis, he who is upon his mound and who is within the place of embalming, the lord of the necropolis, that funerary offerings of bread, beer, and cakes may come forth for him (i.e. the deceased owner).

2. at the Wag-Festival, the Festival of Thoth, the Opening of the Year Festival, the First of the Year Festival, the Festival of Sokar, the monthly festival, and the half monthly festival."

An image of the deceased beneficiary of these texts once appeared in a panel that must have been just to the left of the texts. Below the inscription, seven figures are preserved, each carved in sunk relief and facing toward the viewer's left. Five are identified as lector priests, and the first two, both with short wigs, offer incense and a water fowl to the now-missing image of the deceased owner. The pair is followed by two additional lector priests, and behind them stand three more important figures, to judge from the greater care given to their carving. The first, who may depict the owner's son, wears a long wig and knee-length kilt with a triangular apron panel. The details of both are carefully incised. He also carries a staff. Before him, at the bottom of the vertical text register, stands a diminutive figure (identified as "His son, Sautet") who faces his father. Appearing to be by another hand, he is probably a later addition to the composition. Behind this group, a man identified as the lector priest Nefer-renpet also holds a staff. The final figure is identified as the royal ornament Sautet. She wears a long dress, a collar, and a short wig.

39. PROVENANCE:

Uncertain, but perhaps Asyut, based on the internal evidence provided by the texts.

39. BIBLIOGRAPHY:

Christies (London) 12 December 1990, lot 199, p. 90.

39. LITERATURE:

For two reliefs of comparable date, see Hayes (1953), figs. 87-88, pp. 145-146.

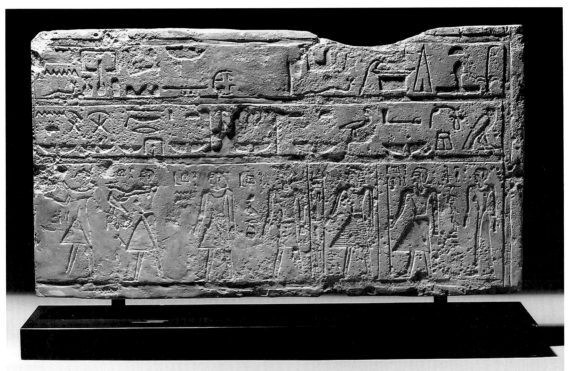

39

71

40. BUST OF A WOMAN

Black granite
Middle Kingdom, Dynasty XII, ca. 1991-1786 B.C.
H. 21 cm. (8 1/4")

Regrettably, the attractive Middle Kingdom sculpture of a woman, perhaps from a seated statue, was broken off at the waist, and the lower portion is missing. She wears a long, full wig with two braids that fall forward over her breasts. The high waist of her shift is indicated just beneath her breasts. Her face is round with emphasized eyes and slightly pursed lips. The ears are also emphasized and are pushed forward by the heavy wig, a common occurrence in the sculpture of the Middle Kingdom.

40. BIBLIOGRAPHY:

G. Scott, *The Past Rediscovered: Everyday Life in Ancient Egypt*, New Haven, 1983, cat. no. 100, pp. 11, 13; Hoffman (1988), cat. no. 90, p. 91.

41. SEATED STATUE OF AN OFFICIAL

An anonymous Middle Kingdom official is shown seated upon a low-backed support in a dignified manner. Both hands are placed flat, palms down, on the apron panel of his knee-length kilt. The official also wears a shoulder-length striated wig of a type associated with the first part of the Twelfth Dynasty (reigns of Amenemhat I-Sesostris II).

During the Middle Kingdom, sculptors favored hard, dark stones, like the black basalt used for this work. Despite the dense stone selected, the sculpture is well carved, and the sculptor has paid attention to the details of the facial features. Probably intended to serve as the principal image in the owner's tomb, it may have been placed in a separate base made from another material. Frequently such separate bases are inscribed with a brief offering text that includes the statue owner's name and titles, and this may account for the fact that the sculpture itself lacks an inscription. Alternatively, the statue has been broken in two at the ankles, and perhaps this occurred in antiquity prior to its completion and the addition of a text.

41. BIBLIOGRAPHY:

Superior (1978), cat. no. 1, p. 9.
Hoffman (1988), cat. no. 89, p. 91.

41. LITERATURE:

For other Middle Kingdom private statues wearing a *shendyt*-style kilt, see Edinburgh 1959.24 in Bourriau (1988), cat. no.18, p. 28 and an example at the MMA in Hayes (1953), fig. 123, p. 206.

74

41 DETAIL

41

41. SEATED STATUE OF AN OFFICIAL

Black basalt
Middle Kingdom, Dynasty XII, ca. 1991-1786 B.C.
H. 38.1 cm. (15")
W. of base: 12 cm.
D. of base: 23 cm.

42. GROUP STATUE

Limestone
Middle Kingdom, Dynasty XII, ca. 1991-1786 B.C.
H. 17 cm. (7")
L. 39 cm.
D. 9.5 cm.

The ancient Egyptian private tomb, whether of grand or moderate design, usually provided sculptural images of the tomb owner and, if possible, additional family members. Whether three-dimensional or two-dimensional, these images were typically identified by inscriptions. To the ancient Egyptians, these images served as an eternal abode for a spiritual aspect of the deceased which could dwell within the tomb.

Five members of a family group, two male and three female, are represented by this sculpture. The man and woman at the viewer's far left are identified by the inscriptions as Ibi and the housewife Ka-es, respectively. They are probably the principal owners of the statue, as they are also named as the beneficiaries of the offering invocations inscribed on the statue base. The male figure in the center is named Hor-wer-nakht, while the female figure to his left seems to be named Mery. The last female figure, that at the viewer's far right, is unidentified.

This statue is typical of both provincial work and of the sculpture of the Middle Kingdom. While the level of workmanship is not high, the craftsman worked in the standard sculptural idiom of his day. The figures are quite compact forms; with full wigs that force the ears forward; the garments serve as an area suitable for inscription, in each case completing the texts begun on the support. These elements are characteristic of the private sculpture of the Middle Kingdom in general. However, the slender, lanky proportions of the figures differ from the robust body types favored by the artists and patrons of the court. Rather, the figures of this group statue are typical of the provincial, almost "folk," tradition employed by regional artists throughout Egypt's long history.

The overall shape of the sculpture suggests that it was once set in a niche. Most probably, this niche would have formed part of the offering place of a private tomb. However, the statue may have been part of a modest private shrine at a cult center such as Abydos or Asyut.

42. PRESERVED COLOR:

Traces of red-brown remain on the flesh of the male figures, and similar traces of yellow remain on the flesh of the female figures. Some white is still retained on the garments.

42. BIBLIOGRAPHY:

Hoffman (1988), cat. no. 88, pp. 90-91.

42. PARALLELS:

Leiden inv. nr. AST 47, see Hans D. Schneider and Maarten J. Raven, *De Egyptische Oudheid*, Leiden, 1981, p. 67, no. 48.

43. STELA
Painted limestone
Middle Kingdom, Dynasty XII-XIII, ca. 1991-1633 B.C.
H. 66 cm. (26")
W. 43.2 cm.

The form of the round-topped stela flourished during the Middle Kingdom and continued to be used in Egypt into the Coptic Period. As an important type of commemorative monument, a stela was generally erected for the benefit of an individual, whether royal or private, and it could serve either a funerary or commemorative purpose.

This stela is of funerary intent; its partially preserved inscription invokes the mortuary deity Anubis to provide offerings of water, beer, and incense for the deceased owner. He is depicted in the upper register seated with his wife, Ty, before various food offerings placed on stands and on the traditional offering mat. An officiant, perhaps the owner's son, performs the offering ritual and pours a libation from the jar held in his far hand. Behind the seated couple stands their daughter, It-ankhu. An interesting detail of the scene is the fan, shown with its palm-column handle turned upward, placed beneath the lion-paw-foot seat.

The lower register shows a similar scene, wherein the standing owners face their offerings, and are accompanied by a larger entourage of three female and two male figures, probably additional members of the owner's household. At the top of the stela, the two eyes of Horus appear, and the whole is encircled by a *kheker* band.

43. BIBLIOGRAPHY:
Sotheby's (New York) 29 May 1987, lot no. 29.

43

44. OFFERING TABLE

Limestone
Dynasty XII, ca. 1991-1786 B.C.
L. 41.8 cm. (16 1/2")
W. 37.4 cm.
D. 4.3 cm.

Offering tables provided a central focus for the ancient Egyptian funerary cult. Placed in an accessible area of the deceased's tomb, such as a chapel or offering niche, the offering table was the designated spot where various beverages, foodstuffs, and incense would be ritually proffered to the spirit of the tomb owner. To ensure that offerings would continue to be available should the cult cease to function, sculptors carved images of the desired offerings onto the surface of the stone, and added the proper inscriptions to ensure a steady "spiritual" supply of offerings would be available for the use of the owner's spirit. The center of this offering table requests one thousand units each of bread loaves, beer jars, cuts of beef and fowl, and articles of alabaster and linen. The symmetrically arranged offering texts inscribed around the outer edge of the offering table are addressed to the funerary deities Osiris and Anubis, respectively, for the benefit of the female owner whose name is Sat-tchenet.

44. PARALLELS:
Bourriau (1988), cat. no. 85, p. 101; Patch (1990), cat. nos. 17, 20, pp. 27, 31-32.

45. KNEELING PAIR STATUE OF SENEDJEM
Painted limestone
New Kingdom, Dynasty XIX, ca. 1303-1200 B.C.
H. 35 cm. (13 3/4")
W. of base: 22.5 cm.
D. of base: 14.2 cm.

During the New Kingdom, the artisans who built and decorated the tombs of the royal family in the Valley of the Kings and the Valley of the Queens at Thebes lived in an isolated village, not far from their places of work, which today is named Deir el-Medina. The area has been excavated and extensively studied and has provided information about the lives of the inhabitants of this ancient village from the archaeological evidence of their tombs, their dwellings, and the royal tombs in which they worked.

The intact tomb of one of the village's most important citizens, the craftsman Senedjem, was discovered in 1886. Senedjem's tomb was excavated and decorated at the beginning of the Nineteenth Dynasty, and he seems to have flourished during the reigns of Seti I and Ramesses II. Although the objects discovered in the tomb were dispersed to a number of institutions and collections, the vibrantly painted tomb contained the mummies of Senedjem; his wife, Iy-neferty; his son, Khonsu; his daughter-in-law, Ta-neket; and a woman named Isis, who was probably also a family member.

The present statue derives from Senedjem's tomb as well, although it was intended to decorate the tomb's exterior. Probably placed in a niche near the top of the tomb's pyramidion, the statue's stela is appropriately inscribed with a sun hymn. The stela is supported by two kneeling figures, and at its top is a solar boat containing the sun's disk and a seated, falcon-headed solar deity. Beneath are eight partially preserved vertical columns of hieroglyphic text surrounding an image of Senedjem kneeling, his hands raised in adoration. Senedjem is depicted wearing a long, full wig, a short chin beard, and a full ankle-length kilt that is belted low on the waist. The text is a hymn to the sun and a brief dedication,

"...[on] the horizon of heaven. Greetings as you rise from the primeval waters and illuminate the Two Lands after you have come forth, (spoken) by the Servant in the Place of Truth, Senedjem, the vindicated. It is his son who causes his name to live, Khonsu. His mother is the Lady of the House, Iy-neferty."

The two figures that support the stela are probably to be identified as Senedjem (statue's right) and his son, Khonsu (statue's left), as the brief label text on the stela's side edge at the sculpture's left suggests, "The Servant of the Lord of the Two Lands, Khonsu, the vindicated, and his sister, the Lady..."[1] Each figure wears a long, shoulder-length wig. Indeed, the two figures are differentiated by artistic convention to represent a youthful and an older subject. The figure at the sculpture's left wears a knee-length kilt belted at the waist and a fashionable double wig, as befits a young man. The figure at the statue's right wears a high-waisted, ankle-length kilt and a wig of anachronistic style, both appropriate for the depiction of an elder gentleman.

45. PRESERVED COLOR:
Red-brown for flesh; black on wigs, boat, and belt of left figure; red on solar disk.

45 VIEW OF BACK

45. BIBLIOGRAPHY:

Bernard Bruyère, *La Tombe No. l de Sen-nedjem*, Cairo, l959, pp. 18-20, pl. XII.
Sotheby's (London) 5 July 1982, lot no. 101.

45. PARALLEL:

Louvre A. 63, see Vandier (1958), pl. CLX, no. 5.

45. LITERATURE:

For a reconstruction drawing of the exterior of a Deir el-Medina tomb chapel with pyramidion, see *Mummies*, fig. 12, p. 24 and Kitchen (1982) ill. no. 63. It is also worth comparing the statue of Men in Hodjash and Berlev (1982) no. 72, pp. 126, 128-131.

45. NOTE:

1. Ramesside pair statues depicting a father and son are known (for example Cairo JE 35257). However, it is also possible that both figures could be intended to represent Senedjem, a not uncommon practice in Egyptian pair statues, particularly those of earlier date.

16

46. STELA OF SHISHAK

Limestone
Late Period, Dynasty XXIV-XXVI, 760-525 B.C.
H. 82.6 cm. (32 1/4")
W. 43.2 cm.

The round-topped funerary stela, first popular during the Middle Kingdom, continued into later periods (Cat. Nos. 43, 145, 146). This example shows the owner, Shishak, son of Djed-khonsu-iuf-ankh, standing with arms raised in adoration while he makes an offering to the funerary deity Osiris and his consort, the goddess Isis. Shishak wears a low-waisted, mid-calf length kilt, a sash over his far shoulder, and a full, shoulder-length wig that is swept behind the ears. Between Shishak and the enthroned Osiris is an offering table supporting bread loaves, cakes, and a lotus blossom. Osiris is depicted in the traditional manner, mummiform and wearing a long divine beard, a broad collar, and a crown with twin plumes and uraeus serpent. He also holds his emblems of royal authority, the crook and flail. Isis wears a traditional, close-fitting sheath dress; long wig; and a crown consisting of cow-horns, sun disk, and uraeus serpent. She holds her near hand aloft in a gesture of support for her resurrected husband, while grasping an *ankh* sign in her far hand. Above this scene is a winged sun disk with two pendant uraeus serpents, while five brief texts serve to label the principals. Below the three figures is an offering text, inscribed in eight horizontal registers, that invokes the composite deity Ptah-sokar-osiris and the funerary deity Anubis. It requests a variety of benefits for the owner's spirit. References to various Memphite locales in the text suggest that the stela was originally erected in a necropolis near ancient Memphis.

47. RELIEF REPRESENTATION OF AN OFFICIAL

A sensitive rendering of an important Late Period official,this relief fragment probably derives from one of the elaborate Theban tombs of officials dating to the late Twenty-fifth and early Twenty-sixth Dynasties. The facial features are carefully carved, and details, such as the elongated eye, the channels of the ear, the well-formed nose, and slightly pursed lips, are worked with sophisticated elegance. A sense of detail is also evident in the remains of the broad collar and suspension cord for an amulet which passes over it. Above the official's head are traces of an hieroglyphic inscription that includes the determinative used in writing the names of cities and towns. Traces of a decorative *kheker* border may also be seen at the far side of the fragment indicating that no additional figures appeared behind the official in the original composition. Interestingly, the facial features are reminiscent of a relief representation of the well-known courtier Harwa, and, although it is not possible to make a positive attribution at this time, the Harer relief must date from the general period of the great Theban officials Harwa, Mentu-em-hat, and Nespekashuti.

47. BIBLIOGRAPHY:

Hoffman (1988), cat. no. 93, p. 94.

47. LITERATURE:

For a relief representation of Harwa in his Theban tomb, see E.R. Russmann, "Harwa as a Precursor of Mentuemhat," *Artibus Aegypti (Studio in Honorem Bernardi V. Bothmer)*, Brussels, 1983, fig. 5.

48. FUNERARY CONES

Tapering clay funerary cones were set in horizontal rows above the entrance of Theban private tombs primarily during the Eighteenth, Nineteenth, and Twentieth Dynasties, although earlier examples dating to the Middle Kingdom and others to the Late Period are known. Funerary cones appear to have been intended to simulate the appearance of wooden roof beams in dwellings, and are typically stamped with the name and titles of the tomb owner. The two examples in the Harer Family Trust collection derive from the tombs of Mermose and Menkheperre-seneb.

48 A. LITERATURE:

Funerary Cones, no. 170. For a view of funerary cones in place, see Wilkinson (1983), ill. no. 10.

49. MUMMY MASK

During the Ptolemaic and Roman periods, cartonnage (individual pieces of painted plaster on linen or papyrus) were placed over specific portions of the mummy. Of these, the most important must surely have been the mask, which covered the head and a portion of the upper chest. The mask was usually fashioned into a conventionalized "portrait" of the deceased, and the face is often gilt, as here, with the eyes and eyebrows rendered in black paint, the white of the eye also being indicated. Similarly common is the long wig with twin braids falling over the breast and the broad collar. This example further shows a diced pattern on the upper portion of the wig, while the braids have been decorated with images closely associated with the mortuary cult. As is often the case with such masks, this example has had some restoration in modern times.

49. BIBLIOGRAPHY:

Hoffman (1988), cat. no. 100, p. 96.

49. PARALLELS AND LITERATURE:

For two masks of similar date, see *Mummies*, cat. nos. 150-151, pp. 201-202.

47. RELIEF REPRESENTATION OF AN OFFICIAL

Limestone
Late Period, late Dynasty XXV-early Dynasty XXVI, ca. 670- 650 B.C.
H. 33.6 cm. (13 1/4")

48 A, B

49

48. FUNERARY CONES

Pottery
New Kingdom, Dynasty XVIII, 1558-1303 B.C.

48 A. MERMOSE

Temp. Amenhotep III, ca. 1397-1360 B.C.
L. 16.5 cm. (6 1/2")
Diam. 5.6 cm.

48 B. MENKHEPERRE-SENEB

L. 18 cm. (7 1/8")
Diam. 6.2 cm.

49. MUMMY MASK

Painted plaster on linen
Ptolemaic Period, 304-30 B.C.
H. 35.5 cm. (14")

50

50. CANOPIC JARS

Limestone with black ink inscriptions
Third Intermediate Period, Dynasty XXI-XXIV, ca. 1085-715 B.C.
Average H. 23 cm. (9 1/16")

During mummification, five internal organs believed most susceptible to decay and most important for the future welfare of the deceased were removed from the body and embalmed. However, only the heart, held to be the seat of the emotions and thought processes, was returned to the body. The intestines, stomach, liver, and lungs were instead placed in individual jars and buried in the tomb near the body. These jars, termed canopic jars, were used from the Old Kingdom until Graeco-Roman times, and evolved from simple, undecorated containers to inscribed vases with lids carved to resemble the heads of the four sons of the god Horus, as shown here. Each of these minor deities was believed to safeguard a particular organ: falcon-headed Qebeh-senuf watched over the intestines, jackal-headed Dua-mutef protected the stomach, human-headed Imsety guarded the liver, and baboon-headed Hapy had charge of the lungs. This set of canopic jars is noteworthy for the animated quality of the carving of the four heads and for the hieratic inscription on each jar. The owner of this set appears to have been named Ankh-payef- heri, son of Mery-re. Both were troop commanders.

51. OSIRIS
Painted gesso on wood
Late Period, Dynasty XXVI, 664-525 B.C.
H. 71.7 cm. (28 1/4")

This strikingly painted figure of the god Osiris is probably associated with the Ptah-sokar-osiris figures used as papyrus containers. They were included in private burials from the Third Intermediate Period until the Ptolemaic Period. The present example is arresting for the marked contrast between the simple, black mass of the body and the brightly colored, detailed head, broad collar, and crown. Both the black of Osiris's body and the green used for his face symbolize fertility and renewed life; these two colors are associated with the annual Nile inundation which carried with it rich silt for the fields of Egypt. Other pigments include white, red, and blue.

51. PROVENANCE:

Ex-collections Drexel, MIA (16.268).

52. SHAWABTI FIGURES AND SHAWABTI COFFIN
Blue-glazed faience figures; limestone coffin
Late Period - Ptolemaic Period, 760-30 B.C.
L. of coffin: 31.1 cm. (12 1/4")
Average H. of figure: 8.5 cm.

The *shawabti* figure was included in the burial of most individuals of sufficient means from the Middle Kingdom until the Ptolemaic period. These figures, usually mummiform in appearance, were intended to serve as substitute workers for their deceased owner, should any manual labor be necessary in the afterlife. Hence, *shawabti* figures are often equipped with hoes and baskets to assist them in such tasks as cultivating fields, transporting sand, excavating irrigation ditches and filling them with water. Since the volume of work that the deceased might be called upon to perform might be high, most tombs contained multiple figures; some owners had 365 figures - one for each day of the year. Often included were an appropriate number of overseers holding flails to see that the allotted tasks were performed. Large groups of *shawabti* figures could be placed in the tomb in stone or wood containers, as were these examples.

52. PROVENANCE:

Ex-collections Drexel, MIA (16.253).

52. LITERATURE:

For a group of shawabti figures in a wooden coffin, see Berlin (1967), cat. no. 925. For a New Kingdom wooden shawabti box and a Late Period example, see *Mummies*, cat. no. 106, p. 156 and cat. no. 125c, p. 175.

52

93

53. SHAWABTI FIGURE

Brown basalt (?)
Middle Kingdom, Dynasty XIII, ca. 1786-1633 B.C.
H. 12.2 cm. (4 3/4")

Small statuettes, occasionally wrapped in linen and placed in a model coffin, began to appear in private tombs during the Eleventh Dynasty. These figures, probably intended to provide a substitute dwelling for the deceased's spirit, are the forerunners of later *shawabti* figures. By the Twelfth Dynasty, they had become mummiform in appearance, and by the close of the Middle Kingdom in Dynasty XIII, the figures seem to have taken on their roles as substitute workers for the deceased owner. One of these late Middle Kingdom figures is represented in the Harer Family Trust collection. This statuette represents late Middle Kingdom *shawabti* figures, as well as late Middle Kingdom sculptural style in general in its use of a hard, dark stone; the treatment of the figure's heavy wig, prominent ears, and "hooded" eyes; and in the emphasis placed on the over-large hands.

53. PARALLELS AND LITERATURE:

See Hayes (1953), fig. 216, p. 328; Aubert (1974), pl. 1, nos. 1-2; Schneider (1977), no. 1.2.4.1; Bourriau (1988), cat. no. 82, p.99; *Mummies*, cat. no. 56, p. 126.

54. SHAWABTI FIGURE

Wood with traces of black ink inscription
Second Intermediate Period, Dynasty XVII, ca. 1650-1558 B.C.
H. 18.8 cm. (7 3/8")

This figure, representative of the crude and peg-like *shawabti* figures made during the troubled times of the Second Intermediate Period, is an interesting link between the funerary practices of the Middle Kingdom and those of the New Kingdom. Its style is rough and folklike; only the essential aspects of form and facial features have been addressed by the ancient carver.

54. LITERATURE:

Petrie (1935/1974), pl. XXIV, nos. 7-10; pl. XXV, nos. 16-29; Newberry (1957), pls. I (47921), III, IV; Hayes (1959), fig. 15, p. 33; Schneider (1977), nos. 2.11.4; 2.1.1.6; 2.1.2.1.

53

54

55

56

55. SHAWABTI FIGURE

Painted wood
New Kingdom, Dynasty XIX, ca. 1303-1200 B.C.
H. 23.8 cm. (9 3/8")

56. SHAWABTI FIGURE

Limestone
New Kingdom, Dynasty XIX, ca. 1303-1200 B.C.
H. 27.5 cm. (11 7/8")

55. SHAWABTI FIGURE

Shawabti figures carried hoes, baskets, and other equipment such as *nu*-pots. *Shawabti* figures were often inscribed with the Sixth Chapter of the *Book of the Dead*, or at least a portion of it. This text details the sort of tasks expected of the figure by its owner and instructs the figure to volunteer for any work that the owner is called upon to perform. A full text appears in crisply carved and carefully painted hieroglyphs on this elegant wooden *shawabti* figure dating to the early Nineteenth Dynasty. Despite its beauty and intricate detail, however, the *shawabti* figure was a ready-made object for the mortuary trade, as its text demonstrates. The text was written in advance with a space left blank for the insertion of the purchaser's name in the appropriate place. In this instance, the name was never added. Regardless, the careful carving of the curls of the double wig, the sensitive rendering of the facial features, and the careful attention to detail throughout (such as the skillfully executed basket placed squarely in the center of the back, complete with netting and suspended *nu*-pots), make this an extremely handsome and appealing example.

55. BIBLIOGRAPHY:

Sotheby's (New York) 19 May 1979, lot no. 90.

55. PARALLELS:

Chappaz (1984), no. 008, pp. 28-29.

56. SHAWABTI FIGURE

Careful attention to detail is evident in this courtly *shawabti* figure. He is shown wearing an elegantly curled double wig with long pendant lappet elements and an elaborately pleated gown with a wrap-around sash. This costume was popular among officials of the later New Kingdom, and the figure's broad facial features are compatible with a date for its carving in the Ramesside Period, probably during the Nineteenth Dynasty. *Shawabti* figures in the dress of the living, rather than shown mummiform, were generally used as overseers for their more mundane fellows. As is typical for the type, the central pleat of the gown's apron panel was inscribed, although the owner's name is regrettably now lost.

56. PRESERVED PIGMENT:

Traces of the following are preserved: red-brown on exposed flesh; black on wig and outlining of feet and toes; white on garment; pink on the garment covering the chest, light "flesh-tone" on the garment covering the abdomen and shoulders.

56. BIBLIOGRAPHY:

Sotheby's (London) 13 December 1977, lot no. 182.

56. PARALLELS:

Schneider (1972), nos. 3.2.7.1; 3.2.7.3; 3.2.8.1. Each of these, like the Harer Family Trust collection examples, preserves on the apron panel of the kilt the beginning and end of a brief inscription, but lacks the owner's name and titles ("The Osiris...the vindicated"). Were the names painted and now lost, have the inscriptions been erased, or were these ready-made shop pieces awaiting inscription of the purchaser's name? See also Newberry (1957), pl. XX (47222).

57A. IY-NEFERTY

Painted limestone
New Kingdom, early Dynasty XIX, ca. 1290 B.C.
H. 19 cm. (7 1/2")

57 B. IUWY

Bichrome glazed white-and flesh-colored faience
New Kingdom, Dynasty XIX, ca. 1303-1200 B.C.
H. 12 cm. (4 3/4")

57 C. HENUT-TAWY

Painted wood
New Kingdom, Third Intermediate Period, Dynasty XXI, ca. 1085-945 B.C.

57 D. DJEDU-MAAT-ISET-ANKH

Painted terracotta
New Kingdom - Third Intermediate Period, Dynasty XX-XXI, ca. 1200-945 B.C.
H. 11.1 cm. (4 5/16")

57 A. LITERATURE:

A *shawabti* figure of Iy-neferty's husband, Senedjem, is in the MMA, see Hayes (1959), fig. 272, pp. 425-426.

57 C. PROVENANCE:

Deir el-Bahari, 1891. Ex-collections Drexel, MIA (16.265).

57 C. PARALLELS:

A second example is in the Harer Family Trust collection, ex-MIA (16.264).

57 D. PROVENANCE:

Ex-collections Drexel, MIA (16.727).

57 D. PARALLELS:

A second example is in the Harer Family Trust collection, ex-MIA (16.732). Two further examples were reportedly in the collection of the Chicago Art Institute and are presumably now housed in the Oriental Institute Museum.

57 A-D

57. SELECTION OF SHAWABTI FIGURES

The grouping of four *shawabti* figures shows the wide range of materials and styles employed during the later New Kingdom and its aftermáth for private burials. The first (57A) belongs to the Lady of the House Iy-neferty, wife of the craftsman Senedjem (see Cat. No. 45), and was discovered in their tomb at Deir el-Medina (Tomb No. 1) in l886. It is elegant in its simplicity, and the white limestone has been sparingly painted to render detail. A multi-color glazed faience *shawabti* figure inscribed for the "Scribe of the Offering Tables of the Lord of the Two Lands, Iuwy," was probably made in imitation of stone models (57B). Similarly, the less costly wooden (57C) and pressed clay (57D) *shawabti* figures presented acceptable substitutes for limestone figures for owners of more limited means.

58 A, B

58. TWO ROYAL SHAWABTI FIGURES
New Kingdom, Ramesside Period, ca. 1303-1085 B.C.

The relative artistic merit of *shawabti* figures was not always based on rank and wealth alone. Many fine *shawabti* figures that survive were made for the royal families of Egypt and Nubia (See Cat. No. 60); kings might also possess less striking, but presumably equally effective, examples. These two *shawabti* figures demonstrate that appropriate form and inscription were adequate to satisfy the demand for an extensive royal work force in the afterlife.

58 A. SETI I
Wood
Dynasty XIX, ca. 1303-1290 B.C.
H. 18.7 cm. (7 3/8")

58 B. RAMESSES VI
Alabaster
Dynasty XX, ca. 1150-1145 B.C.
H. 14 cm. (5 1/2")

58. PROVENANCE:
Thebes, Valley of the Kings.

58 A. BIBLIOGRAPHY:
Christie's (London) 26 November 1980, lot 222.

58 A. PARALLELS:
See Aubert (1974), pp 75-82, pls. 12-13, nos. 27-29; Chappaz (1984), cat. nos. 001, 002, pp. 21-23.

58 B. ADDED COLORS:
Traces of blue and green; black ink inscription and details.

58 B. BIBLIOGRAPHY:
Christies (London) 12 December 1990, lot 188, p. 86.

58 B. PARALLELS:
Newberry (1957), pl. XXXI (48418, 48425); Aubert (1974), pl. 23, no. 49.

59 A

59 B

59 C

Bronze
Third Intermediate Period, Dynasty XXI, ca. 1085-945 B.C.

These three *shawabti* figures are each solid cast bronze, a rare material for the genre. Bronze *shawabti* figures were popular during the Twenty-first Dynasty, the most important examples perhaps being those made for King Psusennes I (fl. ca. 1025 B.C.), who ruled in the Delta and was buried at Tanis (Cat. No. 59A). The other two examples belong to a general who served that king, Wen-djeban-en-djed, who was also buried in the royal necropolis at Tanis.

59 A. PSUSENNES I
H. 8 cm. (3 1/4")

59 B. WEN-DJEBAN-EN-DJED
H. 8.5 cm. (3 3/8")

59 C. WEN-DJEBAN-EN-DJED
H. 8.5 cm. (3 3/8")

59. PROVENANCE:

Tanis.

59 C. LITERATURE:

See Aubert (1974), pp. 153-156, pls. 32-33, 37; Schneider (1977), nos. 4.7.0.9, 4.7.1.7, 4.7.1.2, respectively (Vol. II, pp. 152-154; Vol. III, pl. 56.). For bronze shawabti figures, see also Peter A. Clayton, "Royal Bronze Shawabti Figures," *JEA* 58 (1972), pp. 167-175 and Otto J. Schaden, "A Bronze Ushebty of Pharaoh Psusennes I," *Muse* 18 (1984), pp. 70-73.

60 A

60 B

60 C

60. SHAWABTI FIGURES OF TWO WOMEN NAMED HENUT-TAWY
Blue-glazed faience
Third Intermediate Period, Dynasty XXI, ca. 1085-945 B.C.

Three *shawabti* figures made for two women named Henut-tawy, each a pivotal figure during the Twenty-first Dynasty, demonstrate the subtle differences that may be discerned between shawabti figures. Illustrated are two overseer figures, one with an exceptionally intense blue glaze, and a worker figure. These figures are from Deir el-Bahari, where they were found in the second half of the Nineteenth Century in the so-called Great Cache.

60 A. QUEEN HENUT-TAWY (OVERSEER FIGURE)
H. 12 cm. (4 3/4")

60 B. HENUT-TAWY, DIVINE ADORATRICE (OVERSEER FIGURE)
H. 15.5 cm. (6 1/8")

60 C. HENUT-TAWY, DIVINE ADORATRICE (WORKER FIGURE)
H. 16.5 cm. (6 1/2")

60. PROVENANCE:
Deir el-Bahari.

60 B. PARALLEL:
Newberry (1957), pl. XXXII (48460).

60 C. PARALLELS:
Aubert (1974), pl. 31, nos. 68-69; Schneider (1977), no. 4.3.0.8.

61. SHAWABTI FITURE OF KING SENKAMANISKEN

In antiquity, the land of Kush (Nubia) was heavily influenced by the culture of ancient Egypt, which controlled much of the area during the Middle and New Kingdoms. During the Late Period, however, the situation was briefly reversed and for approximately a century Kushite kings reigned in Egypt, forming the Twenty-fifth Dynasty (760-656 B.C.). The Dynasty's hold over Egypt, however, was brought to a close by invading Assyrians and, as Egypt fell to Assyrian troops, the Dynasty withdrew to its homeland. Senkamanisken ruled only in Kush and was buried in a pyramid tomb at Nuri, where this *shawabti* figure was found together with at least another 409 steatite and 467 faience examples.

The *shawabti* figure closely resembles Egyptian models, and the mummiform statuette shows the figure wearing the royal *nemes* headcloth, double uraeus serpent, and kingly beard. While some *shawabti* figures of Senkamanisken hold the royal crook and flail (overseer figures ?), this example holds traditional hoes in each hand. The figure is inscribed with six horizontal registers of neatly carved hieroglyphs which record a version of the Sixth Chapter of the *Book of the Dead*.

61. BIBLIOGRAPHY:

Christie's (London) 13 July 1983, lot no. 98.

61. LITERATURE:

For a *shawabti* figure holding the crook and flail, compare Brooklyn Museum 39.5, see Wenig (1978), cat. no. 87, p. 175 and Brooklyn (1989) cat. no. 74.

61. PROVENANCE:

Nuri, Pyramid No. 3.

62. SHAWABTI FIGURES OF TCHA-NEN-HABU

During the Late Period, *shawabti* figures were still included in private burials in large numbers. Tcha-nen-habu served as an Admiral in Egypt's royal navy, probably under King Amasis, the last great ruler of the Twenty-Sixth Dynasty. To one side of the entrance to his tomb, 203 *shawabti* figures were found, with an additional 198 figures to the other side of the entrance. Two examples are now in the Harer Family Trust collection.

62. PROVENANCE:

Saqqara, Tomb of Tcha-nen-habu.

62 B. PUBLISHED:

Christie's (London) 31 May 1979, lot no. 150.

62 B. LITERATURE:

Aubert (1974), pp. 227-228, pl. 59, no. 139. For the tomb, see *Topographical Bibliography*, Vol. III (*Memphis*, pt. 2, fasc. II), Oxford, 1979, p. 648.

61

61. SHAWABTI FIGURE OF KING SENKAMANISKEN

Steatite
Kushite, 643-623 B.C.
H. 20 cm. (7 7/8")

62. SHAWABTI FIGURES OF TCHA-NEN-HABU

Green-glazed faience
Late Period, Dynasty XXVI, probably reign of King Amasis,
570-526 B.C.

62 A, B

62 A. SHAWABTI FIGURE
H. 15.9 cm. (6 1/4")

62 B. SHAWABTI FIGURE
H. 19 cm. (7 1/2")

USHABTI FIGURE OF THE SCRIBE
HOR-PTAH-DJED-KA
XXV–XXVI DYNASTY

FOUND AT HAWARA BY PETRIE

63

64

63. SHAWABTI FIGURES OF HORWEDJA AND HOR-PTAH-DJED-KA
Grayish green-glazed faience
Late Period, Dynasty XXX, 378-341 B.C.

These two *shawabti* figures, both discovered at the site of Hawara by Sir W.M.F. Petrie, well demonstrate the high standard of workmanship then possible in the production of this class of funerary statuette. Some 399 *shawabti* figures of Horwedja were excavated. Of this total, 203 figures were aligned in rows in a niche that faced Horwedja's massive stone sarcophagus, while an additional 196 figures were similarly aligned on the opposite wall of the tomb. Most display a high degree of artistic talent in the treatment of the facial features and in a scrupulous attention to detail.

63 A. HORWEDJA
H. 22.8 cm. (9")

63 B. HOR-PTAH-DJED-KA
H. 19 cm. (7 1/2")

63. PROVENANCE:
Hawara.

63 A. LITERATURE:
Petrie (1935/1974), pl. XLII, pos. 547, 549, 55; Aubert (1974), pp. 253-254, pl. 65, fig. 154; Schneider (1977), no. 5.3.1188.

64. WINGED SCARAB PECTORAL
Glazed faience
Third Intermediate Period, Dynasty XXI-XXIV, ca. 1085 B.C.
Total L: 17.1 cm. (6 1/8")

Pectorals of various types were often placed on the breast of the mummy. This example shows a winged scarab beetle, a potent symbol for the ancient Egyptians of the sun's daily rebirth. As such, it was an appropriate amuletic pectoral for inclusion in a burial. This example is in three sections (although the body and wings may not have belonged together in antiquity) and each section is pierced to allow it to be stitched to the exterior of the mummy wrappings.

64. PROVENANCE:
Ex-collections James Ford Bell, MIA (16.722).

64. LITERATURE:
Petrie (1914/1972), no. 93, p. 25, pl. XI; Fazzini (1975), cat. no. 111, pp. 126, 138.

65. AMULETS
New Kingdom - Ptolemaic Period, ca. 1558-30 B.C.

Amulets were important objects for both the living and the dead in ancient Egypt. Made from a wide variety of materials, in a myriad of forms, amulets were believed to provide protection to the owner from both general and specific evils. The *Djed* Pillar, Papyrus Scepter, and Two Fingers amulets were commonly included with burials, while the Eye of Horus amulet was worn both by the living and the dead. Alone, it symbolized the sun and probably safeguarded against the "evil eye," while pairs could represent the two eyes" of the celestial falcon god, the sun and the moon.

65 A. *DJED* **PILLAR AMULET**
Blue-glazed faience
H. 9.3 cm. (3 11/16")

65 B. PAPYRUS SCEPTER AMULET
Blue-glazed faience
H. 4.1 cm. (1 5/8")

65 C. TWO FINGERS AMULET
Black steatite
L. 7 cm. (2 3/4")

65 D. EYE OF HORUS AMULET
Blue-glazed faience
L. 3 cm. (1 3/16")

65 A. PROVENANCE:
Ex-collections Drexel, MIA (16.484).

65 A. PARALLEL:
See Cat. No. 132B.

65 A. LITERATURE:
Petrie (1914/1972), no. 35, p. 15, pl. III.

65 B. PARALLEL:
See Cat. No. 132C.

65 B. LITERATURE:
Petrie (1914/1972), no. 20, pp. 12-13, pl. II; Reisner (1958), pl. XXVII, no. 13009.

65 C. LITERATURE:
Petrie (1914/1972), no. 273, p. 51, pl. XLIII; Reisner (1958), pl. XXIX, no. 1319.

65 D. PARALLEL:
See Cat. No. 1M.

65 D. LITERATURE:
Petrie (1914/1972), no. 138, pp. 32-33, pls. XXIV-XXV.

65 C

65 B

65 A

65 D

66 A-G

66. AMULETS IN ANIMAL FORM
New Kingdom - Ptolemaic Period, ca. 1558-30 B.C.

Because of the close relationship that certain cult animals shared with their associated deities, small animal statuettes were popularly worn as amulets and donated as votive gifts. The falcon was identified with the solar gods Horus and Re, the ram with the creator gods Amen and Khnum, and the baboon with the god of writing and measurement, Thoth. The mortuary deity Anubis was identified with the jackal, a scavenging animal that no doubt was often seen near the fresh, shallow burials of commoners, while the composite hippopotamus deity Ta-weret (whose name literally translates as 'The Great One') was a goddess appropriately identified with pregnancy and child birth. Occasionally, certain cult animals received particular veneration in their own right, as was the case for the Apis bull. Upon death, each Apis bull was accorded an elaborate funeral, and numerous votive images of these sacred animals survive.

66 A. APIS BULL AMULET
Green-glazed faience
L. 2.5 cm. (1")

66 B. RAM AMULET
Grayish blue-glazed faience
L. 4 cm. (1 9/16")

66 C. FALCON AMULET
Green-glazed faience
H. 3.8 cm. (1 1/2")

66 D. ANUBIS AMULET
Green-glazed faience
H. 6.2 cm. (2 5/8")

66 E. TA-WERET AMULET
Grayish green-glazed faience
H. 5.1 cm. (2")

66 F. BABOON
Greenish blue-glazed faience
H. 5.1 cm. (2")

66 G. BABOON HOLDING AN EYE OF HORUS
Grayish blue-glazed faience
H. 3 cm. (1 3/16")

66 B. PROVENANCE:
Ex-collections Drexel, MIA (16.136).

66 B. PARALLEL:
Reisner (1958), pl. XXLL, no. 12587.

66 C. PROVENANCE:
Ex-collections Drexel, MIA (16.92).

66 F. PROVENANCE:
Ex-collections Drexel, MIA (16.78).

66 G. BIBLIOGRAPHY:
Sotheby's (New York) 21 May 1977, lot no. 322.

111

67. SEKHMET
Blue-glazed faience
Third Intermediate Period, Dynasty XXI-XXIV, ca. 1085-715 B.C.
H. 6.3 cm. (2 1/2")

The lion-headed goddess Sekhmet (see Cat. Nos. 25, 68A, 68C l04, l05) sits upon a throne and holds a ceremonial musical instrument associated with religious ritual called a sistrum. Iconographically, the small statuette is closely related to the relief pendant of the same goddess in the next entry (Cat. No. 68A).

67. PROVENANCE:
Ex-collections Drexel, MIA (16.63).

67. PARALLEL:
Münzen und Medaillen (Basel) 27 June 1974, lot no. 91.

68. PLAQUE AND PENDANTS
Glazed faience
Third Intermediate Period - Ptolemaic Period, ca. 1085-30 B.C.

The faience plaque (Cat. No. 68B) was mounted on another object, probably fashioned from wood, in antiquity. Decorated with the image of Maat, goddess of righteousness and universal order, it perhaps once decorated a shrine or chest, possibly used in the temple or mortuary cults. It retains traces of gilding. One of the pendants showing Sekhmet (Cat. No. 68A) depicts her holding a sistrum as in the previous entry (Cat. No. 67); the other shows her accompanying Onuris (Cat. No. 68C).

68 A. SEKHMET PENDANT
H. 3.6 cm. (1 7/16")

68 B. MAAT PLAQUE
H. 8.3 cm. (3 1/4")

68 C. SEKHMET PENDANT
H. 4.9 cm. (1 7/8")

68 A

68 B

67

68 C

69 A-C

70

114

69. AMULETS OF ANTHROPOMORPHIC DEITIES
Late Period - Ptolemaic Period, 760-30 B.C.

Small figures of Egypt's gods were also made in large numbers from faience. They probably served as amulets and votive objects, and typically are cast with a loop for suspension. Included in the present group are miniature representations of the goddess Isis suckling her son Horus, and Shu, god of the air. Bes, a dwarf deity with a mask-like face, was closely linked with domestic matters.

69 A. SHU AMULET
Glazed faience
H. 3.5 cm. (1 3/8")

69 B. ISIS AND HORUS AMULET
Greenish blue-glazed faience
H. 5.1 cm. (2")

69 C. BES AMULET
Light blue-glazed faience
H. 3.1 cm. (1 1/4")

70. NATURALISTIC MUMMY MASK
Painted plaster
Roman Period, 2nd Century A.D.
H.25 cm. (9 7/8")

Traditional Egyptian burial customs were mixed with those of the larger Mediterranean in Egypt at the close of its ancient history. While the Egyptian custom of mummification continued to be practiced on both native Egyptians and foreigners of sufficient means, a trend toward a more naturalistic treatment of the mummy mask emerged, particularly for the many Greek residents of the Faiyum. A naturalistic approach is evident in the facial features of this mummy mask of a woman, which appear to derive more from the artistic traditions of the Graeco-Roman world than from the artistic conventions of ancient Egyptian funerary art. The naturalism of this mask has been heightened by the use of applied pigment.

70. PROVENANCE:
Ex-collection Alfred von Jurits, Vienna.

71. MUMMY MASK OF A WOMAN

Painted stucco
Roman Period, lst-2nd century A.D.
H. 49.5 cm. (19 1/2")

A more stylized naturalism is evident in this exuberantly decorated mummy mask. Made of sculptured stucco and enhanced by paint, the woman's hair, floral fillet, jewelry, and breasts have been worked three-dimensionally. She also wears a broad collar, below which appear two jackals, each perched on a shrine, flanking a somewhat misunderstood *djed* pillar.

71. PARALLELS:

For a similar floral fillet and the treatment of the eyebrows, see Berlin (1967), cat. no. 1026. For a particularly fine example of the type, see MMA 19.2.6 in Thompson (1982), fig. 2.

72. HIGH RELIEF CARVING OF A DEVOTEE OF ISIS

Painted limestone
Roman Period, 4th century A.D.
H. 49.8 cm. (19 1/8")

A series of small stelae depicting children as followers of Isis has been identified with the Roman site of Antinoe. Typical of the group is this example which shows the child seated on the ground in an asymmetric pose. He holds what appears to be a bunch of grapes in the left hand and a bird in the right. The figure is recessed to create a niche-like stela, and the facial features conform to the conventions of the group, including the triangular shape of the face with its emphasized, highly stylized eyes.

72. PROVENANCE:
Perhaps Antinoe.

72. PARALLELS AND LITERATURE:

John D. Cooney, "An Early Christian Sculpture from Egypt," *Brooklyn Museum Annual* 2-3 (1963), pp. 37-47; de Bourguet (1967), pp. 95, 98, 123-124, fig. 24; Allard Pierson Museum (Amsterdam), no. 8726; illustrated in Allard Pierson Museum, *Selected Pieces*, Amsterdam, 1976, pp. 30-31; Ede (1983), pg. 90, no. 238.

71

72

73. SCULPTURE OF A MAN

Painted limestone
Romano - Coptic, 4th-5th century A.D.
H. 55.3 cm. (21 3/4")

Apart from its material and its probable funerary function, any real relationship to ancient Egypt's long sculptural tradition has been superceded in this figure of a man carved in very high relief. Instead, the artistic tradition most evident is that of the Graeco-Roman world, and the sculpture could be compared to provincial work from widely divergent points in the Roman Empire. Consistent with Egyptian artistic output of the Roman Period, however, are the emphasized eyes and the garland held in the left hand. These elements may be seen not only in funerary sculpture, but also in the near-contemporary Faiyum portraits and sculptural mummy masks.

73. PARALLELS:

Certain elements, such as the garland held in the sculpture's left hand, are paralleled in the Faiyum portraits. See John D. Cooney, *Pagan and Christian Egypt*, Brooklyn,1941, cat. nos. 6, 9, 10; Thompson (1982), figs. 9, 27, 28, 38, 39, 42.

74. POTTERY VESSELS

Romano - Coptic, 30 B.C.- A.D. 500

During the Roman Period, pottery fashioned in Egypt tended to imitate wares produced elsewhere in the Roman world. The large flask (Cat. No. 74A) was probably used as a container for beer or wine. Pilgrim flasks with simple, stamped decoration were popular souvenirs purchased by pilgrims at the shrines of Egypt's Christian martyrs. The shrine of St. Menas in the desert east of Alexandria was renowned for its springs, whose waters produced miraculous cures. There, pilgrims purchased small terracotta flasks stamped with the saint's image to carry a sample of the water away with them.

74 A. FLASK

H. 25.4 cm. (10")

74 B. ST. MENAS FLASK

H. 8.3 cm. (3 1/4")

74 C. ST MENAS FLASK

H. 10.4 cm. (4 1/8")

74 A. PROVENANCE:

Ex-collections Drexel, MIA (16.578).

74 C. PROVENANCE:

Ex-collections Place, MIA (25.345).

74 C. LITERATURE:

For St. Menas flasks, see du Bourguet (1967), pp. 86, 93, fig. 17; Bourriau (1981), cat. nos. 188-189, pp. 95-96.

75. ANIMAL FIGURINES
Terracotta
Ptolemaic Period - Roman Period, 2nd century B.C. - 2nd century A.D.

As early as the Twenty-sixth Dynasty, craftsmen trained in the artistic traditions of ancient Greece worked in Egypt. Hellenistic influence rapidly increased following the absorption of Egypt into the empire created by Alexander the Great and, after Rome annexed Egypt in 30 B.C., the traditional art forms of pharaonic Egypt dwindled rapidly. Small-scale sculpture in terracotta, an important Hellenistic medium, was practiced in Egypt, particularly in centers of Hellenistic culture. These small animal figurines are typical of the type and are interesting in the choice of subject matter, since neither the dog nor the pig were popular subjects for Egyptian artists.

75 A. DOG
L. 10.5 cm. (4 1/8")

75 B. PIG
L. 5.7 cm. (2 1/4")

75 A. PROVENANCE:
Ex-collections Place, MIA (25.234).

76. CHARACTER HEADS
Ptolemaic Period, 330-30 B.C.

Figurines of actors, grotesques, and characters of national and personality types were popular products for Hellenistic coroplasts and other artists. These two heads, one of a balding man, the other of a Nubian, are representative of the genre.

76 A. BALDING MAN
Terracotta
H. 4.7 cm. (1 7/8")

76 B. NUBIAN
Plaster
H. 4.5 cm. (1 3/4")

76. PROVENANCE:
Ex-collections Place, MIA (28.24.122; 28.24.162, respectively).

74 A

73

74 B, C

76 A, B

75 A, B

77

78

77. ISIS AND HORUS STATUETTES
Terracotta
Roman Period, 1st century B.C. - 2nd century A.D.

The cult of the goddess Isis was widespread throughout the Roman Empire and was maintained in Egypt into the Fifth Century A.D. While the motif of the mother nursing her son continued the ancient Egyptian tradition, details of costume, pose, and iconography were altered to reflect Hellenistic taste. The reddish color of these terracottas is typical of the Nile clay.

77 A. STATUETTE
H. 12.7 cm. (5")

77 B. STATUETTE
H. 6.3 cm. (2 1/2")

77. PROVENANCE:
Ex-collections Place, MIA (25.211; 25.208, respectively).

78. HORUS FIGURES
Terracotta
Roman Period, 1st century B.C. - 2nd century A.D.

Horus, son of Isis, maintained his popularity in Egypt as well as the rest of the Roman Empire. However, he assumed the appearance of a plump Roman infant, rather than the slender, athletic child of Egyptian tradition. Represented as the child god seated on a phoenix (Cat. No. 78A), the composition is wholly Hellenistic, with only the pose of the finger held to the mouth reminiscent of Egyptian iconography.

78 A. HORUS ON A PHOENIX
H. 8.3 cm. (3 1/4")

78 B. HORUS THE CHILD
H. 10.7 cm. (4 1/4")

78. PROVENANCE:
Ex-collections Place, MIA (25.213, 25.327, respectively).

79. HEAD OF SERAPIS
Plaster
Ptolemaic Period - Roman Period, 2nd century B.C. - 2nd century A.D.
H. 8.3 cm. (3 1/4")

Serapis was a composite deity introduced to the Egyptian pantheon by Ptolemy I in order that both his Egyptian and Greek subjects might have a common god to worship. Combining aspects of the Egyptian divinities Osiris and the Apis Bull with characteristics of the Greek deities Zeus, Dionysos, and Asclepius, the cult of Serapis rapidly spread beyond the boundaries of Egypt. Although not as universally popular as the cult of Isis, temples were dedicated to Serapis throughout the Roman Empire, including one at York in Roman Britain.

79. PROVENANCE:
Ex-collections Place, MIA (28.24.137).

80. FEMALE HEAD FROM A STATUETTE
Terracotta
Ptolemaic Period - Roman Period, 2nd-1st century B.C.
H. 8.2 cm. (3 1/4")

80. PROVENANCE:
Ex-collections Place, MIA (28.24.88).

81. BES
Terracotta
Roman Period, 1st-3rd century A.D.
H. 11.4 cm. (4 1/2")

During the Roman period, the Egyptian deity Bes attained a degree of popularity among the Roman troops stationed along the Nile, and images of him became increasingly militaristic (Cat. Nos. 120, 121). Votive objects of many types depicting Bes, including terracotta figures such as this example, therefore remained common during the Roman Period.

81. PROVENANCE:
Ex-collections Place, MIA (25.217).

79

81

80

TEMPLE, TOMB AND DWELLING:
EGYPTIAN ANTIQUITIES FROM THE HARER FAMILY TRUST COLLECTION

PART II

TEMPLE, TOMB AND DWELLING:
EGYPTIAN ANTIQUITIES FROM THE HARER FAMILY TRUST COLLECTION
Part II

INTRODUCTION

An important aspect of ancient Egyptian culture is religion and systems of religious belief. The lines which today separate the secular from the devotional were less rigid in antiquity if they existed at all. Religious beliefs were an integral part of society and, in this light, it is useful to draw a comparison between ancient Egypt and medieval Europe, where the church and the established patterns of religious belief were equally prevalent throughout the social order. This does not reduce the complex society of ancient Egypt to one which was morbidly bound by religion, but rather notes that objects which modern viewers find to have aesthetic or decorative interest may have presented a series of meanings to the ancient artisan and patron that are now elusive.

In ancient Egypt, religious belief and doctrine linked the realm of the gods to the king and his court and each, in turn, to the sphere of the people. The gods created and sustained life, whether from the celestial realm that observed the affairs of human kind in life, or from the netherworld, which offered the hope of resurrection to renewed life after death. Hence, the gods controlled the welfare of both the living and the dead. However, well-being could be assured, it was believed, through the proper observation of cultic duties, especially by the king. The monarch's role was essential, for the ancient Egyptian king was held to be divine and to partake of a divine essence. As such, he served as an intercessor between his people and the gods and, upon death, was reunited with the divine realm. While living, it was the king's duty to serve as principal officiant, and the temples contained three-dimensional and two-dimensional representations of the pharaoh performing priestly duties, presenting offerings to the gods, or taking part in religious processions (Cat. Nos. 82-85).

The king's activities in essence created a sort of contractual arrangement between himself and the gods on behalf of the people. Pharaoh would see that the temple cult was maintained for the benefit of the gods, and the deities would ensure Egypt's natural order and prosperity in response to proper propitiation. This did not, however, preclude individuals making direct contact with the divine, particularly when they had their own special petitions and problems. Just as royal religious practice is preserved in statues, relief sculpture, and wall paintings, so too has a record of personal piety and devotion on the part of commoners been recovered through the discovery of various sorts of objects.

One important class is votive objects, such as the model ear in the Harer Family Trust collection (Cat. No. 98). It may have been deposited at a temple shrine to ensure that the deity heard the petitioner's prayer or left as a record of an injury or a cure. Other objects donated to shrines as gifts to the gods include small statuettes of deities, their cult animals, and their sacred symbols cast in metal or in faience. In addition, during the later periods of Egyptian history, the bodies of animals sacred to particular gods were mummified and presented to the temples as votive gifts. The Harer Family Trust collection (Cat. Nos. 31, 32, 34, 35, 104, 112, 113, 115-117, 134) holds examples of these votive objects.

The three spheres of the gods, the king, and the people also played a part in the funerary practices of ancient Egypt. Tombs and their contents could be supplied by pharaohs to devoted courtiers, but even where the monument had been privately commissioned, the offering texts inscribed thereon typically began with the ritualistic phrase, "An offering which the king gives..." The doctrine behind the practice presumably recognized the central role of the pharaoh as intercessor, as well as that of rightful owner of the bounty of the realm and so, too, the proper authority to direct its allocation. The actual meaning of the offering text appears to have developed into a concept of shared offerings in which the king theoretically presented an offering to a god and the deity then allowed offerings to revert to the deceased beneficiary. Funerary customs in ancient Egypt also advanced to the level that allowed the deceased to be identified with the revitalized god Osiris (Cat. Nos. 89, 141) and so be resurrected to renewed life.

On the domestic front, the gods played an equally important role, although certain deities were more appropriately invoked there than others. One such was Bes, characteristically portrayed as a dwarf with mask-like features (Cat. Nos. 116, 120, 121). This popular deity was associated with children, childbirth, sexuality, music, dance, and other domestic matters.

It may be seen, then, that objects which reflect patterns of religious belief in ancient Egypt were created for use within each of the three architectural settings dominating the social life of that culture: the temple, the tomb and the dwelling. Statues and relief sculpture adorned temples and important tombs alike. An extensive array of specialized funerary equipment such as canopic jars, *shawabti* figures, and the various trappings associated with the mummy were placed in the tomb. Amulets and small representations of Egypt's gods, their cult animals, and their cult symbols were worn by the living and the dead in ancient Egypt and so were to be encountered in the temple as votive objects and in the tomb and dwelling as amulets and charms. Finally, objects of daily use, including handsome cosmetic containers and implements associated with the household, were ultimately destined to accompany their deceased owner to the netherworld and be lodged in the eternal home, the tomb.

The many references to religious beliefs and symbolism found in what has survived of ancient Egyptian material culture, particularly the many articles directly associated with the funerary cult, may suggest that the ancient Egyptians were both obsessed by religion and that they were morbidly fascinated with death. The literature of ancient Egypt, in concert with the visual arts, supports a different interpretation. Rather, the ancient Egyptians were enthralled with life, and their religious and funerary practices sought to ensure its benefits for the living and its continuation into eternity for the dead.

This is evidenced in the writings and objects associated with ancient Egyptian medicine and medical practice. This topic is especially appropriate for exploration as many objects in the Harer Family Trust collection are related to ancient Egyptian health care. As might be expected, the primary concerns for ancient Egyptian medicine appear to have been the banishment of disease, the healing of injuries, and the prolongation of life.

Medical practitioners in ancient Egypt were varied. Basic terms survive that may be translated as doctor and dentist, as well as phrases that denote a range of medical specializations. Some were already employed by both male and female officials during the Old Kingdom. In addition, the priests of the goddess

Sekhmet, a deity well represented in the Harer Family Trust collection (See Cat. Nos. 25, 104, 105), were credited with medical knowledge, and there were doubtless other, more humble, members of society who assisted with childbirth and with coping with injury and disease. As might be anticipated, certain deities were also important to issues of health and the continuation of life. Min, an ithyphallic deity (Cat No. 115) was no doubt invoked for fertility as were the mother goddesses Hathor and Mut. Ta-weret, whose name translates as "The Great One" and who appeared in the form of a large-bellied hippopotamus, was invoked during pregnancy and childbirth, as was the dwarf deity Bes. The Harer Family Trust collection (Cat. Nos. 113, 116, 120-124) has many images of both.

Egyptian medicine relied on the topical application of various materials to external wounds and injuries or the ingestion of assorted substances to bring about the desired results. The ancient Egyptian pharmacopeia was quite broad, but it is poorly understood at present because so many of the items listed still evade translation and identification. Many of the prescriptions call for a base of honey, beer, or wine. It has been shown that honey has certain medicinal qualities when applied to external wounds, and perhaps the alcohol content of some prescriptions mildly reduced the patient's anxiety if taken internally. Copper compounds, used primarily for eye cosmetics and occasionally for topical application, have been shown to have some anti-bacterial effects, but it is unclear whether they benefited the ancient patient.

It may be that opium was used for medicinal purposes by the Egyptians by the time of the New Kingdom. A type of small pottery vessel, initially imported to Egypt from Cyprus, and resembling the opium poppy grown on that island, seems to support such a conclusion (Cat. Nos. 21D, 126). However, recent scientific tests on the remains of the contents of these vessels are inconclusive in proving that they ever contained an opiate. Of course, pottery vessels, especially foreign wares containing imported products, were reused in ancient times, but there is no evidence that the Egyptians were familiar with opium until the Graeco-Roman era.

Interestingly, however, the ancient Egyptians did have access to a mood-altering substance other than alcohol. This was in the form of the Egyptian Lotus (*Nymphae*), which exhibits narcotic properties. Indeed, Egyptologists owe Dr. Harer a debt of thanks for his research in this area and for introducing this intriguing issue to the literature of Egyptology. [1]

In addition to the archaeological evidence of medical practices in ancient Egypt, medical papyri provide an important source of information. Egyptian medicine was renowned throughout the ancient world, and the early papyri found at Kahun and dating to the Middle Kingdom show that ancient Egyptian medicine relied both on methods of a rational and practical nature and on those more closely related to sympathetic magic and religious ritual. The renowned Edwin Smith Surgical Papyrus is a prime example of the former. It deals with injuries that might have been sustained by the military or by heavy construction workers and presents a series of "case histories" that are organized in a logical order, from head injuries downward. They are further arranged such that for each area the cases move from least to most serious and so reflect the physician's ability to treat the patient. Overall, the Edwin Smith Surgical Papyrus presents ancient Egyptian medicine at its most "scientific." The physician visually and manually examined each wound, establishing the type and condition of the injury, made a diagnosis and prescribed a treatment. The ancient Egyptians were keen observers of their natural world and took a practical and functional approach to life. It is these very traits that emerge from the methodology of the Edwin Smith Surgical Papyrus.

The ancient health care system also comprised religious belief and sympathetic magic. This approach is demonstrated by the many amulets worn in life and in death by the ancient Egyptians, as well as the so-called healing stelae, several of which are in the Harer Family Trust collection (Cat. Nos. 106, 110, 111). The latter were intended to ward off venomous bites and stings but may have had other benefits. Their basis is perhaps in Egyptian mythology, which relates that Osiris, the rightful ruler of all Egypt, was slain by his jealous brother Seth, who tried to usurp the throne. Osiris's wife, Isis magically revivified the corpse and conceived an heir, their son Horus. The child eventually assumed the kingship but endured many trials and difficulties in the process. One such involves a venomous bite from which he was cured by his mother's magic. As Robert S. Bianchi has noted,[2] Horus appears in an apotropaic capacity as early as the Pyramid Texts, and it is believed that these healing stelae represent a late development of the tradition. It is assumed that a liquid was poured over the stelae and then consumed to protect those who partook from snakes, scorpions, and other such dangerous creatures. The healing stelae in the Harer Family Trust collection well exemplify that images were used by the populace as the naively worked examples demonstrate.

In addition to reflecting ancient Egyptian religious belief, funerary ritual, medical practices, daily life, and the interrelationship between the realm of the gods, that of the king, and that of the people, many objects in the Harer Family Trust collection provide insights for the visual arts of ancient Egypt. Some demonstrate the Egyptian sculptor's virtuosity in working hard, intractable stone (Cat. Nos. 25, 82). Others illustrate the Egyptian palette and conventions of two-dimensional representation (Cat. Nos. 26, 146). Still others demonstrate the working methods and materials of Egyptian artists (Cat. Nos. 8-18) or the vocabulary of ancient Egyptian folk art. In addition, the Harer Family Trust collection contains many small scale works which invite close observation and reveal the range of artistic accomplishment achieved by the ancient Egyptian artisan when working in miniature. A careful inspection of such objects as the steatite *Head of a King* (Cat. No. 95), the *Falcon-headed Solar Deities* (Cat. Nos. 102A-B), and the inlaid *Osiris* (Cat. No. 89) demonstrates the monumentality and power of even the smallest works, works which are compelling in their balance of intricate detail and striking simplicity.

Gerry D. Scott, III

[1]W. Benson Harer, Jr. "Pharmacological and Biological Properties of the Egyptian Lotus, *JARCE* XXII (1985), pp. 49-54.

[2]Brooklyn (1982), cat. no. 99.

82. STANDARD-BEARING STATUE OF A QUEEN, POSSIBLY NEFERTIRY

Black granite
New Kingdom, Dynasty XIX, reign of Ramesses II, ca. 1290-1223 B.C.
H. 94 cm. (37")
H. of standard: 91.8 cm.
H. of back pillar: 87.8 cm.
H. of face: 10.4 cm.
H. of face on standard: 3.9 cm.
D. of break: 28.2 cm.

Unquestionably the most important work of ancient Egyptian art in the Harer Family Trust collection, this extraordinary sculpture depicts a queen who lived during the reign of Ramesses II. She is shown as a participant in a temple procession, and she strides forward with her left leg advanced. A sacred standard is cradled in her left arm, its top graced by a bust of the goddess Mut, consort of the principal state deity Amen. Mut's face is framed by her heavy wig, surmounted by the double crown and uraeus serpent, and the staff of the standard is inscribed. Partially preserved, it reads in its entirety, "The good god, the son of Amen, born of Mut in order to rule all that the sun's disk encircles, the lord of the Two Lands, User-maat-re Setep-en-re (Ramesses II)..." [1]

This queen is remarkable as a standard-bearing statue, a popular form of temple sculpture during the New Kingdom that was primarily restricted to male owners. The only other female example of Ramesside date known to the author is a partially preserved sculpture now in Budapest. [2]

The present example shows the queen wearing a heavy wig of carefully carved curls, over which is a vulture headdress. Such a headdress is appropriate, for the vulture, as a symbol of female divinity, was closely associated with both queens and the goddess Mut, whose name was written with a vulture hieroglyph. In addition, the queen wears a pair of disk-shaped earrings, a broad collar, a bracelet on her right wrist, an elegantly pleated gown, and sandals. The gown is fringed at its closure and is held in place by the knotted tie incised between, and just below, the breasts. The queen also holds a folded handkerchief in her right hand.

The now missing statue base probably identified this royal lady, but the sculpture is otherwise well preserved. Only the queen's nose and left forearm show losses, and the surface of the stone continues to reflect the contrasting levels of polish favored by Ramesside sculptors. The queen's face, neck, and hands are more polished than the elements of the costume and draw the viewer's attention directly to the royal countenance. There is a similar contrast in the facial features of the bust of Mut on the standard in relation to her crown and headdress. The differing degrees of surface polish that so strikingly set off the queen's flesh from her attire reflect the ancient sculptor's mastery of form and meticulous attention to detail. This is also evident in the treatment of the elaborately pleated gown which reveals the lithe proportions and graceful motion of the body beneath it, while painstakingly recording the garment's various details.

Since the queen's name has not been preserved on the sculpture, it is impossible to identify the ancient owner with certainty at present. Three queens, each an important figure in the life of Ramesses II, have been suggested: his mother Tuya, his chief queen and wife Nefertiry, and his daughter Merit-amen, who was elevated to her mother's position as chief queen following Nefertiry's death. A sculptural image of each queen survives, but owing to significant differences in scale, ancient Egyptian

82

conventions of portraiture at the time, and the likelihood of family similarities, a comparison of the facial features in this case proves illusory.

The Mut imagery of the sculpture's iconography, and Mut's role as consort to the state god Amen, is similarly problematic in helping to identify the queen. Since the text states that Ramesses II is the son of Amen and that he was born of Mut, an argument might be made that the queen should be identified with Tuya, Ramesses II's mother. However, such phrases are rather standard and are an integral element of ancient Egypt's religious concept of the divinity of kingship. Hence, the inscription should probably not be taken as explicitly representing the degree of filiation between the statue owner and Ramesses II. The sculpture more probably represents either of Ramesses II's principal queens, Nefertiry or Merit-amen, despite Mut's standing as a mother goddess, for the queen represented would hold the same relationship with Ramesses II that the goddess Mut maintained as consort to the state god Amen. In this light, a comparison of the Harer Family Trust sculpture with the small-scale representation of Nefertiry in a group statue of the youthful Ramesses II in turn reveals similarities, notably in the treatment of the eyes, the expression of the mouth, and the presentation of the relationship between the gown and the female form beneath it.

82. PROVENANCE:

Ex-collection Pitcairn (The Lord's New Church), Bryn Athyn, PA.

82. LITERATURE:

For the statue of Tuya, Vatican 22, see Vandier (1958), pl. CXXXV, no. 2 and K.A. Kitchen, *Pharoah Triumphant*, Warminster, England, 1982, p. 96, fig. 32; for the Turin group statue showing Nefertiry, Turin 1380, see Ernesto Scamuzzi, *Egyptian Art in the Egyptian Museum of Turin*, New York, 1965, pls. LVII, LIX; for the recently discovered statue of Merit-amen, see Y.S.S. al-Masri, "Preliminary Report on the Excavations in Akhmim by the Egyptian Antiquities Organization," *Annales du Service des Antiquités de l'Egypte*, LXIX (1983), pls. I, III; for another important, but also unidentified, queen of Ramesses II (CG 600),see Vandier (1958), pl. CXXXVI, no. 2 and Saleh 1987), cat. no. 208 (attributed to Merit-amen).

82. NOTE:

[1]The final signs lend themselves to two interpretations, due to the preservation of the text. The cartouche may well be followed by the standard epithet, "beloved of Amen-re," however, the sun disk for "-re" more closely resembles the bread loaf for "*t*" and is quite flat on the bottom. Similarly, the possible horizontal "*mr*" sign also resembles the "*nb*" sign, and an alternate, although unusual, reading of "beloved of Amenet, lady of..." may be possible.

[2]For the Budapest statue, see Szepmuveszeti Muzeum, *Egyptomi Kiallitas*, Budapest, 1976, no. 23, p. 40.

83

83. RELIEF DEPICTION OF A GODDESS OR DIVINE ADORATRICE
Sandstone
Late Period - Ptolemaic Period, 760-30 B.C.
H. 52.1 cm. (20 1/2")

82. BIBLIOGRAPHY:

José Pijóan, *Summa Artis*, Vol. III, *El Arte Egipcio*, Madrid (1932), p. 278, fig. 363.
Vandier 1958), pl. CLXIX, no. 7.
Christie's (New York) 15 June l979, lot no. 189.
John Herbert (ed.) *Christie's Review of the Season 1979*, London, p. 421.
Cyril Aldred, *Egyptian Art*, New York, 1980, p. 186 (identified as Nefertiry).
Helmut Satzinger, "Der Heilige Stab als Kraftquelle des Konigs," *Jahrbuch der Kunsthistorischen Sammlungen in Wien*, 77 (1981), p. 33 (Dok. B4).
Ch. Desroches-Noblecourt, "Touy, Mère de Ramesses II, la Reine Tanedmy et les Réliques de l'Expérience Amarnienne," *L'Egyptologie en 1979*, Vol. II, Paris, 1982, pp. 238-239, fig. 65 (identified as Tuya).
Catherine Chadefaud, *Les Statues Porte- ensignes de l'Egypt Ancienne*, Paris, 1982, p. 98 (PEC. 4).

83. DESCRIPTION:

The female figure faces the viewer's left; her partially missing far arm is raised, while her near arm hangs at her side. She wears a vulture headdress with two rising plumes which suggests that she may be a consort of the god Amen (either Mut or Amenet), or perhaps his Divine Adoratrice, an important female clerical position. Three vertical columns of hieroglyphic text are partially preserved; two behind the figure, and one before her. Interestingly, a parallel may be provided by a relief depicting the Divine Adoratrice Nitocris preserved in Moscow. The pose and headdress closely mirror those of the Harer Family Trust collection's relief, although the figure's proportions are quite different.

83. PARALLEL:

Hodjash and Berlev (1982), no. 112, pp. 166, 171.

84. DESCRIPTION:

The head of a male deity, apparently Onuris, faces the viewer's left. The carving is accomplished, and the facial features are sensitively worked. The deity wears a simple, flat crown from which plumes once rose, and a broad collar and necklace at his throat.

84. PROVENANCE:

Perhaps Behbeit el-Hagar, Temple of Isis or Samanoud.

84. PARALLELS:

WAG 22.5, see Steindorff (l946), no. 255, pp. 75-76, pl. LXIV.

84

84. RELIEF HEAD OF A DEITY

Granite
Ptolemaic Period, temp. Ptolemy II-III, 284-222 B.C.
H. 24.8 cm. (9 3/4")

86 A

85

86 B

85. RELIEF REPRESENTATION OF KING AKHENATEN

Limestone
New Kingdom, Dynasty XVIII, reign of Akhenaten, ca. 1370-1353 B.C.
L. 33 cm. (13")

85. DESCRIPTION:

The damaged features of King Akhenaten are partially preserved on this limestone block, carved in sunk relief. He wears a tall crown, probably the Blue Crown, and a single lappet from it is visible at the back. Sun rays, emanating from a now-missing Aten, are also visible below the crown.

85. PROVENANCE:

Hermopolis.

85. LITERATURE:

For a similar treatment of the lappet, see *Schimmel*, cat. no. 243.

86. TWO AMULETS

Silver

86 A. BABOON

New Kingdom - Third Intermediate Period, ca. 1558-715 B.C.
H. 1.9 cm. (3/4")

86 B. NEPHTHYS

Late Period - Ptolemaic Period, ca. 760-304 B.C.
H. 2.3 cm. (7/8")

87

88

89

90

87. SATIS

Silver
Third Intermediate Period, Dynasty XXI-XXIV, ca. 1085-715 B.C.
H. 6.8 cm. (2 5/8")

87. PROVENANCE:

Ex-collections Place, MIA (27.14).

87. DESCRIPTION:

Satis, goddess of Elephantine and consort of the creator-god Khnum, wears the White Crown of Upper Egypt decorated with gazelle horns and a miniature ram's head. The latter symbolizes Khnum, and it is surmounted by a scorpion. The figure is solid cast.

88. BABOON

Silver and serpentine
Late Period, Dynasty XXV-XXXI, ca. 760-330 B.C.
H. 5.4 cm. (2 1/8")
Weight: 91.97 grams (approximately 10 *Kedet*)

88. COMMENTS:

This baboon may have been one of a type used as a weight or as an element on a votive balance scale. This baboon's association with Thoth, god of writing and measurement, makes the animal's form ideally suited for such a purpose.

88. LITERATURE:

For a discussion of silver-headed, small-scale Egyptian sculpture, see Beate George, "Thoth als Ibis und Pavian," *Medelhavsmuseet Bulletin*19 (1984), pp. 39-48.

89. OSIRIS

Bronze with inlays of gold and copper
Late Period, Dynasty XXVI-XXXI, 664-330 B.C.
H. 20 cm. (7 7/8")

89. DESCRIPTION:

An extremely fine, solid-cast statuette, the god Osiris is depicted mummiform. He holds the crook and flail, and wears the *atef* crown, divine beard, and broad collar. The plumes of the crown, the braids of the beard, and the three strands of the collar are inlaid with gold wire, while the eyes, the chin strap of the beard, and the crook display an inlay of copper or a variant copper alloy different from the material used for the rest of the statuette. This latter technique, using copper or variant copper alloy to produce a contrasting color to bring out detail, is uncommon in Egyptian bronze sculpture, although the use of gold, silver, and electrum as inlays is more frequently encountered. The figure's rectangular plinth bears a brief dedicatory inscription in incised hieroglyphs. It reads in part, "A statement by Osiris-Wenenefer, [I] give protection, health, joy, goodly prosperity...to Hor...tef-nakht."

90. STATUETTE OF HORUS THE CHILD

Black serpentine
Late Period - Ptolemaic Period, 664-30 B.C.
H. 3.6 cm. (1 3/8")

90. DESCRIPTION:

Only the upper portion of this statuette is preserved. The treatment of the face and other details such as the sidelock mark it as a product of fair quality.

91. HORUS THE CHILD SEATED ON A LION THRONE

Bronze
Late Period - Ptolemaic Period, 664-30 B.C.
H. 10.7 cm. (4 1/8")

91. PROVENANCE:

Ex-collections Place, MIA (28.24.36).

91. DESCRIPTION:

Horus, the divine son of Osiris and Isis, is depicted in the traditional manner of a child, nude with one finger held to his mouth. Despite this, he is to be identified with royal authority, as his crown and lion throne indicate.

91. BIBLIOGRAPHY:

Sotheby's (New York) 19 May 1979, lot no. 37.

91

92

93

92

92. HORUS THE CHILD SEATED ON A LION THRONE

Steatite
Meroitic (?), ca. lst century B.C.
H. 17 cm. (6 11/16")

92. DESCRIPTION:

This representation of the divine child Horus, is also nude, with right index finger held to his mouth. He wears the Double Crown and sidelock of youth. Behind him is a diminutive figure of his mother Isis, who supports him with her arms and her wings. The lions forming the sides of the throne display manes of a characteristic, apron-like form, and the back of the throne shows an unusual treatment. Dr. Robert S. Bianchi, of the Brooklyn Museum, has suggested that the work may be Meroitic and date to the first century B.C.

92. PARALLELS:

BM EA 69535, ill. in "Museum Acquisitions 1984," *JEA* 72 (1982), pl. VII, no. 2; CG 38.212 (*Statues de Divinités*, pl. XI). For small-scale lion thrones, see Berlin (1967), cat. no. 827 (bronze); Münzen und Medaillen (Basel) 16 June l981, lot no. 110.

93. NUDE MALE FIGURE

Wood
New Kingdom, Dynasty XVIII-XX, ca. 1558-1085 B.C.
H. 10.5 cm. (4 1/8")

93. DESCRIPTION:

This striding statuette, missing its lower legs and feet, shows the owner as an older child or youth. While he is nude and wears the sidelock, his hands are held to his sides, rather than having a finger held to the mouth. Some attention has been paid to the carving of the facial features and to the forms of the body, and the workmanship is of a fairly high quality. The figure may be Horus the Child, but the lack of a royal attribute may indicate that the statuette is better assigned to a private owner.

93. PROVENANCE:

Ex-collection Science Museum of Connecticut, Hartford (54.857).

93. BIBLIOGRAPHY:

Bolton Gallery (Boston) 17 October 1987, lot no. 187C.

93. LITERATURE:

For a New Kingdom nude youth, see Hayes (1959), fig. 30.

94. CHILD KING

Bronze
Late Period - Ptolemaic Period, 664-30 B.C.
H. 4.6 cm. (1 7/8")

94. DESCRIPTION:

A charming miniature statuette, the figure depicts a child king, presumably in the guise of Horus the Child, seated on the ground with his legs drawn up toward his chest. His left hand rests on the left knee, while the right hand grasps the crook scepter. The young king wears a Double Crown with single uraeus serpent, but is otherwise nude.

95. HEAD OF A KING

Steatite
New Kingdom, Dynasty XVIII, temp. Amenhotep III -
Tutankhamen, ca. 1397-1343 B.C.
H. 3 cm. (1 1/8")

95. DESCRIPTION:

This small-scale, but exquisitely carved, royal head depicts a youthful ruler of the late Eighteenth Dynasty, perhaps Tutankhamen. He wears the Blue Crown with its disk-shaped decoration, uraeus serpent, and band, each carefully detailed. The sensitive rendering of the facial features reflect the period's penchant for slightly almond-shaped eyes, and the king's neck displays the twin flesh folds so characteristic of late Eighteenth Dynasty depictions of royalty. The high back pillar and slight forward thrust of the neck suggest that the head comes from a small striding statuette of the king.

95. PARALLELS:

For similar heads, see WAG 22.222 in Steindorff (1946), no. 103, p. 40, pl. XIX; Münzen und Medaillen (Basel) 28 April 1972, lot no. 40.

95. LITERATURE:

For sculptural depictions of King Tutankhamen, see Hayes (1954), figs. 185-186.

94

95

95

96. AMULETS
Blue-glazed faience
New Kingdom - Ptolemaic Period, ca. 1558-30 B.C.

96 A. TEMPLE PYLON
H. 2.1 cm. (13/16")

96 B. SHRINE OR CHAPEL
H. 2.5 cm. (1")

96 C. TRUSSED SACRIFICIAL OX
L. 2.5 cm. (1")

97

96 A

98

96 B

96 C

96. LITERATURE:

Petrie (1914/1972), no. 63, p. 20, pl. V; Reisner (1958), pl. XXIX, no. 13342.

97. VOTIVE MODEL OR OFFERING TRAY

Terracotta
Late Period - Ptolemaic Period, 760-30 B.C.
L. 15.9 cm. (6 1/4")

97. COMMENTS:

An enigmatic object, it is difficult to determine its exact function. Although roughly shaped in the form of an offering tray, the presence of two relief crocodiles on its surface, in proximity to the other ten "offerings" of amorphous shape (possibly consisting of two frogs and eight fish), might favor an interpretation as a votive. However, an entrance channel or pouring spout, surmounted by a crudely formed head, appears on the narrower side of the object, suggesting that it received or distributed poured libations.

97. PROVENANCE:

Ex-collections Place, MIA (25.266).

97. PARALLEL:

A very close parallel for this object was seen on the Paris art market in 1991.

98. VOTIVE EAR

Wood
New Kingdom - Ptolemaic Period, ca. 1558-30 B.C.
L. 8.5 cm. (3 3/8")

98. PROVENANCE:

Ex-collections Place, MIA (29.17.33).

98. COMMENTS:

This well-carved, life-size ear is typical of votive gifts left by pious petitioners at healing shrines in ancient Egypt. Presumably the donor presented this object to the shrine that his petition might be heard by the deity (perhaps a request that the sense of hearing might be restored), or in thanksgiving for an answered prayer (such as recovery from a hearing loss or ear affliction).

98. LITERATURE:

For a related type of votive object, the so-called "stelae with ears," see Saleh (1987), cat. no. 221; *EGA*, cat. no. 416, p. 305.

99. FINIAL
Bronze
Late Period - Ptolemaic Period, 760-30 B.C.
H. 12.7 cm. (5")
L. 10.6 cm.

99. DESCRIPTION:

A human-headed scorpion figure surmounts the capital of a papyrus column to create what probably served as the finial of a wood support or staff. The female head wearing a long wig identifies the image as the scorpion goddess Selquet, and it is likely that the finial once crowned an item of temple furniture or a ceremonial accoutrement.

99. PARALLEL:

WAG 54.546, see Steindorff (1946), no. 703, p. 154, pl. CIV.

100. AMULET OF A DIVINE TRIAD
Glazed faience
Late Period - Ptolemaic Period, 760-30 B.C.
H. 3.3 cm. (1 1/4")

100. DESCRIPTION:

Horus the Child is depicted walking between the goddesses Isis and Nephthys. The three hold hands.

101. FALCON AMULET
Glazed faience and silver
New Kingdom - Ptolemaic Period, ca. 1558-30 B.C.
H. 2.1 cm. (13/16")

101. DESCRIPTION:

A solar falcon, either Horus or Re, made from green-glazed faience, sports a silver White Crown, perhaps suggestive of an identification with Horus of Edfu.

102. FALCON-HEADED SOLAR DEITIES
Green-glazed faience
Late Period - Ptolemaic Period, 760-30 B.C.

102. DESCRIPTION:

These amulets, in fact detailed miniature statuettes, represent the striding figure of a falcon-headed solar god, either Horus or Re. In one example, the deity is crowned with a sun disk and uraeus serpent, and wears a wig and royal *shendyt* kilt. The other wears the Double Crown with similar wig and kilt. For both, the wig and kilt have been carefully incised with lines to denote the strands of hair and pleats of the garment, respectively. Each has a back pillar.

102 A. FALCON-HEADED SOLAR DEITIES
H. 3 cm. (1 3/16")

102 B. FALCON-HEADED SOLAR DEITIES
H. 2.5 cm. (1")

100

101

99

102 A

102 B

103

104 A

104 B

103. HORUS RISING FROM A LOTUS BLOSSOM

Glazed faience
Ptolemaic Period, 304-30 B.C.
H. 3 cm. (1 3/16")

103. COMMENTS:

This miniature amulet shows Horus the Child, symbolizing the newly born sun, rising from the primeval waters on a lotus blossom.

104. SEKHMET STATUETTES

Glazed faience
Late Period - Ptolemaic Period, 760-30 B.C.

104. COMMENTS:

These two statuettes, cast with loops for suspension, each depict a lion-headed goddess, probably Sekhmet. It is interesting to compare their proportions. Cat. No. 104A shows the traditional slender female proportions of Egyptian artistic convention, while Cat. No. 104B is notably more voluptuous, perhaps reflecting a foreign stylistic influence. This latter statuette is drilled at the top of the wig to accommodate a decorative headdress of another material.

104 A. SEKHMET STATUETTE

H. 7.3 cm. (2 7/8")

104 A. PROVENANCE:

Ex-collections Drexel, MIA (16.69).

104 B. SEKHMET STATUETTE

H. 6.3 cm. (2 1/2")

104 B. PROVENANCE:

Ex-collections Drexel, MIA (16.72).

105. PLAQUE AND PENDANT DEPICTING SEKHMET NURSING HORUS

Glazed faience
Late Period - Ptolemaic Period, 760-30 B.C.

105. DESCRIPTION:

In each case, a lion-headed goddess, presumably Sekhmet, sits upon a throne and nurses a youthful ruler, either Horus or the pharoah in the guise of Horus. The plaque (Cat. No. 105A) is pierced in two places to allow for its attachment to another object, while the pendant (Cat. No. 105B) was cast with a suspension loop at the back of the lioness head.

105 A. PLAQUE DEPICTING SEKHMET NURSING HORUS

H. 7 cm. (2 3/4")

105 B. PENDANT DEPICTING SEKHMENT NURSING HORUS

H. 3.9 cm. (1 1/2")

106. CIPPUS OF HORUS

Serpentine
Ptolemaic Period, 304-30 B.C.
H. 8.3 cm. (3 1/4")

106. DESCRIPTION:

Horus the Child, nude and wearing the sidelock of youth, shows his mastery over the dangerous forces of nature as he strides forward on the backs of two crocodiles while holding two venomous snakes in each hand. Above his head, the mask-like face of the apotropaic domestic deity Bes appears, while other figures and symbols, carved in relief, surround him. Fifteen horizontal registers of hieroglyphic text, reading right to left, cover the flat back surface of this small sculpture.

106. COMMENTS:

Cippus of Horus sculptures were used to protect their owners from noxious and harmful creatures including snakes, crocodiles, scorpions, and lions. Horus first assumed the role of protector against such natural dangers as early as the Old Kingdom, but it was not until the Late Period that sculptures similar to this example appear. It is conical in its design and may be compared with others of varying quality, some true masterpieces, like the Metternich Stela (MMA 50.85) or Brooklyn 60.73, and others quite crude in style (Cat. No. 110A-B). It is thought that these images may have been activated by pouring a liquid libation over them. The liquid, which was believed to have absorbed the magical efficacy of the hieroglyphic texts and sculptural images, was in turn drunk by, or poured over, the beneficiary to ward off evil. Alternatively, the image may have been touched in some fashion to aid the healing process after an injury had been sustained.

106. LITERATURE:

For Brooklyn 60.73, see Fazzini (1975), cat. no. 124, pp. 127, 138; Brooklyn (1988), cat. no. 99, pp. 204-205; and Brooklyn (1989), cat. no. 88. For numerous healing stelae in Moscow, see Hodjash and Berlev (1982), pp. 244-274; for those in the WAG, see Steindorf (1946), pp. 163-170, pls. CVIII-CIX; and for an important example in Cairo, see Saleh (1987), cat. no. 261.

107. PLAQUE SHOWING HORUS THE CHILD AND A SERPENT

Grayish green-glazed faience
Third Intermediate Period - Ptolemaic Period, ca. 760-30 B.C.
H. 5.6 cm. (2 1/4")

107. DESCRIPTION:

This hieroglyphic-like depiction of Horus the Child shows him nude, with youthful sidelock. A large snake partially encircles the divine figure, and it is likely that this plaque served an apotropaic purpose similar to the Cippus of Horus sculpture, above (Cat. No. 106).

108. PLAQUE SHOWING A KING TREADING ON CROCODILES

Blue-glazed faience
Ptolemaic Period - Roman Period, 2nd century B.C. - 1st century A.D.
H. 3 cm. (3/8")

108. DESCRIPTION:

A nude king, wearing the *nemes* headcloth, treads on the backs of two crocodiles while holding a knife in each hand. The iconography suggests that the royal figure is to be identified with the god Horus, and the object's purpose is probably similar to the apotropaic function intended for Cat. Nos. 106-107 and 109-111 by their ancient owners.

108. LITERATURE:

Compare a Meroitic pendant now in Boston, BMFA 24.781; Wenig (1978), cat. no. 107, p. 191.

109. AMULETS

Glazed faience
Late Period - Ptolemaic Period, 760-30 B.C.

109 A. SERPENT

L. 2.5 cm. (1")

109 A. LITERATURE:

Petrie (1914/1972), no. 58, pp. 18-19, pl. IV.

109 B. CROCODILE

L. 3.8 cm. (1 1/2")

105 A

105 B

106

107

109 A

108

109 B

110. HEALING STELAE

Limestone
Ptolemaic Period - Roman Period, 2nd century B.C. - 1st century A.D.

110. COMMENTS:

The crude workmanship of these examples mark them as items produced in the folk tradition for use by those of limited means. Nonetheless, each maintains the essential elements of the iconography of the type. The nude child god with sidelock treads upon two crocodiles while holding a venomous snake in each hand. Above his head, the mask-like face of Bes appears, while snakes decorate the sides; the back attempts to approximate the stela design of better examples.

110 A. HEALING STELA

H. 9.2 cm. (3 5/8")

110 B. HEALING STELA

H. 11.2 cm. (4 5/8")

110 B. PROVENANCE:

Ex-collections Place, MIA (25.184).

111. HEALING STELA

Serpentine
Ptolemaic Period, 304-30 B.C.
H. 6.2 cm. (2 1/2")

111. DESCRIPTION:

The miniature round-topped stela shows a composite deity carved in raised relief. The god grasps a divine *was*-scepter and a miniature lion in his far hand, while holding a flail in his near hand. He is flanked by four wings, the top pair supported by additional arms.

112. LION-HEADED DEITY

Glazed faience
Late Period - Ptolemaic Period, 760-30 B.C.
H. 5.7 cm. (2 1/4")

112. COMMENTS:

While statuettes of lion-headed goddesses are fairly common, those of lion-headed gods are rare. This example shows reasonably good workmanship, has a suspension loop, and wears an elaborate crown.

110 A

111

110 B

112

113. TA-WARET AMULETS
Green-glazed faience
Third Intermediate Period, Dynasty XXI-XXIV, ca. 1085-715 B.C.

113. COMMENTS:

These two statuettes of the goddess Ta-weret (See also Cat. Nos. 66E, 135A) are interesting to compare. One (Cat. No. 113A) is a typical representation of the deity, who offered protection during childbirth, in the guise of a hippopotamus. The other (Cat. No. 113B) is a more unusual, but equally traditional, representation that shows a composite figure comprised of hippopotamus torso and head, lion's legs and paws, and a stylized crocodile tail. Also of interest is the tiny crocodile perched atop Ta-weret's wig.

113 A. TA-WARET AMULET
H. 6.7 cm. (2 9/l6")

113 A. PROVENANCE:
Ex-collections Drexel, MIA (16.68).

113 B. TA-WARET AMULET
H. 6.7 cm. (2 9/16")

113 B. PROVENANCE:
Ex-collections Drexel, MIA (16.64).

113 B. BIBLIOGRAPHY:
Sotheby's (New York) 20-21 November 1975, lot. no. 406.

114. SEXUAL AMULETS
Blue-glazed faience
Late Period - Roman Period, 760 B.C. - A.D. 200

114. COMMENTS:

These two amulets are related to sexual fertility. Cowrie shells, both natural and manufactured in various materials, were worn in ancient Egypt as early as the Predynastic Period. Their shape, reminiscent of female genitalia, caused them to be associated with sexuality and fertility. The fist fetish, probably symbolic both of male potency and of sexual union, is not often encountered before the Graeco-Roman era.

114 A. COWRIE SHELL
L. 2.5 cm. (1")

114 A. LITERATURE:

Reisner (1958), pl. XXV, nos. 12831, 12832.

114 B. FIST FETISH
L. 2.7 cm. (1 1/4")

114 B. LITERATURE:

Petrie (1914/1974), no. 13, p. 11, pl. I.

115. MIN
Bronze
Late Period - Ptolemaic Period, 664-30 B.C.
H. 8.7 cm. (3 1/2")

116. DANCING BES
Bronze
New Kingdom, Dynasty XVIII-XX, ca. 1558-1085 B.C.
H. 11.4 cm. (4 1/2")

116. DESCRIPTION:

The dwarf god Bes is represented playing a stringed instrument and dancing atop a papyrus column in this unusual statuette. Of particular interest is the pose of the legs in which the right leg bears the body's weight. This sort of pose, essentially the contraposto of the Greeks, is occasionally encountered in minor works, especially those of the late Eighteenth Dynasty.

114 A

114 B

115

116

118

117 A-C

166

117. STATUETTES OF DEITIES
Bronze
Late Period - Ptolemaic Period, 664-30 B.C.
H. 11.4 cm. (4 1/2")

117 A. IAH OR KHONSU
H. 10 cm. (3 15/16")

117 A. PROVENANCE:

Ex-collection Pitt-Rivers.

117 B. IMHOTEP
H. 9.7 cm. (3 7/8")

117 C. SNAKE-HEADED DEITY
H. 11.4 cm. (4 1/2")

118. MOTHER AND NURSING CHILD ON BED
Limestone
New Kingdom, Ramesside Period, Dynasty XIX-XX, ca. 1303-1085 B.C.
L. 35 cm. (13 3/4")
W. 12 cm.

118. DESCRIPTION:

The composition consists of a nude female figure lying on her back on a bed equipped with a footboard. She nurses a nude male child and wears a heavy wig with one large braid brought forward over her right shoulder to rest on her right breast. Her right hand cups her left breast to the child's mouth, while she cradles him to her side with her left arm.

118. PARALLELS:

Brooklyn 14.606, see J.H. Breasted, *Egyptian Servant Statues*, New York, 1947, p. 96, no. 5, pl. 93C. For other examples in Berlin, Munich, and Hanover, see Bodil Hornemann, *Types of Ancient Egyptian Statuary*, vols. IV-V, Munksgaard, 1966, pls. 1292-1296.

119. DESCRIPTION:

The nude female figure stands with her legs together and her arms held to her sides. A full and luxuriant coiffure falls about her shoulders in ringlets and extends to the elbows. Details of the anatomy, including the facial features, fingers, and toes, are indicated.

119. BIBLIOGRAPHY:

Christie's (London) 16 July 1986, lot. no. 256.

120. DESCRIPTION:

A late interpretation of the Egyptian god Bes, this example displays large round eyes surmounted by a continuous brow ridge, a broad nose, and extended ears. The usual feather headdress has been partially broken away, and a round shield appears at the left shoulder. The arms are diminutive, as is the chest, while the head, abdomen, and upper thighs are emphasized.

120. N.B.

The author is indebted to Dr. James F. Romano, of the Brooklyn Museum, who suggested to the Harers that this image of Bes dates to the 2nd-3rd century A.D.

121. DESCRIPTION:

Another late representation of Bes shows the dwarf god holding a knife in his right hand and a serpent in his left. The mask-like face is executed with considerably more skill than was shown by the previous example in terracotta (Cat. No. 120). The large eyes are especially arresting with the arching brows which curl around to the base of each ear. A subsidiary female figure faces Bes. The figure is nude, wears a simple wig surmounted by a cap with feather, and plays a hand-held drum or tambourine. The figure's far leg is elevated, presumably executing a dance step.

121. BIBLIOGRAPHY:

Sotheby's (New York) 2 June 1984, lot no. 68; Sotheby's (New York) 8-9 February 1985, lot no. 242.

121. PARALLELS:

See Hodjash and Berlev (1982), no. 196, pp. 266-274; Rembert Watermann, *Bilder aus dem Lande des Ptah und Imhotep*, Cologne, 1958, ill. no. 56; *Vereniging van Vrienden Allard Pierson Museum Amsterdam*, no. 39, April 1987, ill. no. 23; inv. nr. 7947.

121. N.B.

The author is grateful to Dr. Robert S. Bianchi, of the Brooklyn Museum, who provided Dr. Harer with some of the parallels cited.

119

119. STATUETTE OF ISIS-APHRODITE

Terracotta
Roman Period, 1st century B.C. - 1st century A.D.
H. 32.6 cm. (12 15/16")

120

120. BES

Terracotta
Roman Period, 2nd-3rd century A.D.
H. 39.9 cm. (16 1/8")

121

121. RELIEF REPRESENTATION OF BES

Limestone
Roman Period, 2nd century A.D.
H. 29.5 cm. (11 5/8") L. 29.9 cm

122. BES VASE

Terracotta
Roman Period, lst century B.C. - 3rd century A.D.
H. 14.9 cm. (5 7/8")
Diam. at lip: 4.6 cm.

122. DESCRIPTION:

The body of this broad jar with tall neck and ring foot displays the distinctive facial features and diminutive arms of the god Bes. These elements are in applied relief with some details incised. Since Bes was a beneficent deity whose special domain was the household, his image is most appropriate for domestic pottery. Because Bes was also concerned with the protection of children and of women in childbirth, as well as with matters of sexuality and fertility, vessels such as this might have served a magico-medical function.

122. LITERATURE:

For late Bes vases, see Bourriau (1981), cat. no. 54, p. 38.

123. BES FLASK

Black-glazed faience
Ptolemaic Period, 304-30 B.C.
H. 4.1 cm. (1 5/8")

123. PROVENANCE:

Ex-collections Place, MIA (25.265).

124. BES PENDANTS

Glazed faience
Late Period - Ptolemaic Period, 760-30 B.C.

124. PROVENANCE:

Ex-collections Drexel, MIA (16.75, 16.281, respectively).

124 A. BES PENDANT

H. 4.4 cm. (1 3/4")

124 B. BES PENDANT

H. 4.4 cm. (1 3/4")

125. AMULETS IN THE FORM OF FLASKS

Glazed faience
New Kingdom - Late Period, ca. 1500-300 B.C.

122

124 A

123

124 B

125A   125 B

125 A.   MINIATURE "PILGRIM" FLASK
H. 2.3 cm. (7/8")

125 B.   MINIATURE "NEW YEAR " FLASK
H. 1.7 cm. (5/8")

125 B.   LITERATURE:

For examples of full-scale flasks of both types, see Berlin (1967), cat. nos. 611-613; for a full-scale New Year's flask in the Brooklyn Museum (37.337E), see Riefstahl (1968), cat. no. 60, p. 62.

126.   BASE RING-WARE JUGLETS
Terracotta
New Kingdom, Dynasty XVIII, ca. 1558-1303 B.C.

126.   COMMENTS:

Cypriote base-ring ware juglets appeared in Egypt during the Second Intermediate Period, and the form continued its popularity until the close of the Eighteenth Dynasty. In addition, the vessel type was copied by Egyptian potters, and examples survive made from the distinctive Nile silt of Egypt. These juglets may have contained opium, as their bulbus shape suggests the opium poppy, but scientific tests of the remains of their contents have yet to support this theory conclusively.

126 A.   BASE RING-WARE JUGLET
H. l4 cm. (5 1/2")
Diam. at lip: 3.6 cm.

126 B.   BASE RING-WARE JUGLET
H. 13.8 cm. (5 7/16")
Diam. at lip: 3.6 cm.

126 B.   LITERATURE AND PARALLELS:
See cat. no. 21D and *EGA*, cat. no. 65, p. 84.

126

127. JARS, MORTAR AND PESTLE
Alabaster
Late Period - Ptolemaic Period, 760-30 B.C.

127 A. ALABASTRON
H. 20.3 cm. (8")

127 A. PROVENANCE:
Ex-collections Drexel, MIA.

127 B. ALABASTRON
H. 9.5 cm. (3 3/4")

127 C. MINIATURE VASE
H. 7.6 cm. (3")

127 D. MORTAR
H. 6.4 cm. (2 1/2")

127 E. PESTLE
L. 8 cm. (3 1/8")

127 E. COMMENTS:
Although the mortar and pestle may not have formed a set in antiquity, various types of containers, palettes, and grinding stones used in the preparation of cosmetics, medicines, delicacies, and magico-religious substances are known. This pestle is noteworthy in that it was initially intended as an alabastron. For some reason, perhaps an accident in the carving, it was not completed and instead served as a small grinding stone.

127 E. PARALLELS:
See Vandier d'Abbadie (1972), nos. 593-544, pp. 138-139. For an Eighteenth Dynasty example, see *EGA*, cat. no. 127.

127 A-E

128 A-F

128. SELECTION OF WEIGHTS
Basalt
Late Period, Dynasty XXVI-XXXI, ca. 664-330 B.C.

128. COMMENTS:

Weights were used throughout ancient Egypt's long history. Occasionally, weights were made in a special form, (see Cat. No. 88 for a possible example), but the "cake" type, shown here, was much more typical.

128. PROVENANCE:

Ex-collections Drexel, MIA (16.548).

128 A. WEIGHT
Diam. of base: 7.6 cm. (3")
Weight: 960.7 grams

128 B. WEIGHT
Diam. of base: 6.1 cm. (2 3/8")
Weight: 173.3 grams

128 C. WEIGHT
Diam. of base: 4.4 cm. (1 5/8")
Weight: 46.7 grams

128 D. WEIGHT
Diam. of base: 2.5 cm. (1")
Weight: 19.4 grams

128 E. WEIGHT
Diam. of base: 1.6 cm. (3/8")
Weight: 9.1 grams

128 F. WEIGHT
Diam. of base: 1.5 cm. (3/8")
Weight: 9.0 grams

128. LITERATURE:

See W.M.F. Petrie, *Glass Stamps and Weights, Ancient Weights and Measures*, London (1926, re-issued Warminster, 1974), pls. III-V.

130

129

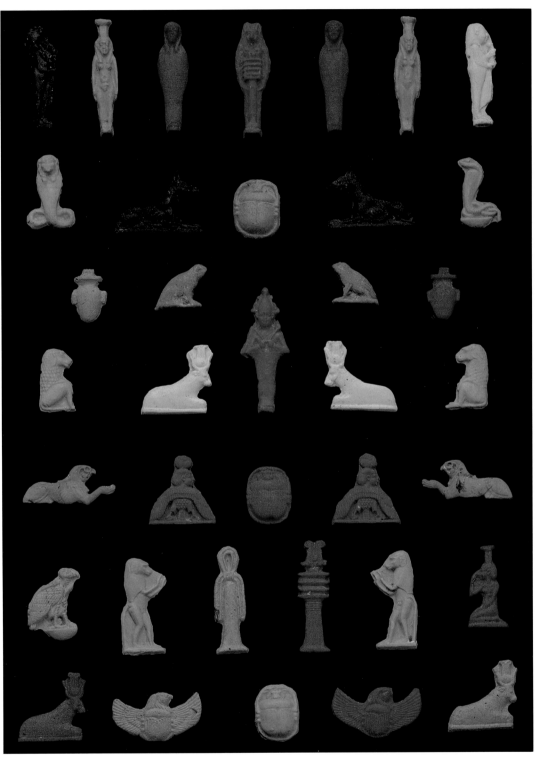

131

129. MODEL STORAGE JARS
Green-glazed faience
Late Period, Dynasty XXVI-XXXI, 664-330 B.C.
L. 14.3 cm. (5 5/8")

129. PROVENANCE:
Ex-collections Place, MIA (25.271).

130. STATUETTE OF A BREWER
Limestone
Old Kingdom, Dynasty VI, ca. 2345-2181 B.C.
H. 9.8 cm. (3 7/8")
L. 12 cm.

130. DESCRIPTION:
A brewer kneels over a vat in this small servant statuette. The upper arms merge with the upper surface of the vat to indicate that they are immersed in its contents. There is minimal detail, but the face, wig, kilt, and lip of the vat are indicated.

130. BIBLIOGRAPHY:
Hoffman (1988), cat. no. 87, p. 90.

130. PARALLEL:
Louvre E.17238; see Raymond Weill, *Dara*, Cairo, 1958, p. 65, no. 79, pl. XXXIX (a).

131. AMULETIC INLAYS
Glazed faience
Late Period, Dynasty XXVII-XXXI, 525-330 B.C.
H. of central Osiris figure: 5.4 cm. (2 1/8")

131. DESCRIPTION:

This mounted collection of thirty-seven inlays depicts various deities and amuletic symbols which were intended to decorate a wooden coffin. The figures, glazed in white, red, yellow, pale green, blue, and black, include Osiris and Nephthys, while jackals, baboons, cows, frogs, and snakes probably are meant to represent the deities Anubis, Thoth, Hathor, Heqat, and Wadjet, respectively. In addition to mummiform figures, the vulture goddess Mut, scarab beetles, falcon-headed sphinxes, and human-headed falcons, the *djed* pillar, knot of Isis, and heart amulet are also represented in the collection.

131. PROVENANCE:

Ex-collection feu Omar Pacha Sultan.

131. BIBLIOGRAPHY:

Collection de feu Omar Pacha Sultan Le Caire, Paris, 1929, no. 632.

131. PARALLELS:

Compare examples found in Reisner (1958), pls. XXVIII, XXX, XXXI.

132 A

132 B

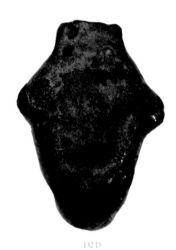

132 C

132. SELECTION OF AMULETS
Glazed faience
Late Period - Ptolemaic Period, 760-30 B.C.

132 A. DOUBLE *SA* **AMULETIC SPACER BEAD**
H. 2.5 cm. (1")

133

132 D

132 A. BIBLIGRAPHY:
Malter & Co. (Los Angeles) 26 February 1978, lot. 110.

132 A. LITERATURE:
Petrie (1914/1972), no. 88, p. 23, pl. VII.

132 B. *DJED* **PILLAR AMULET**
H. 2.5 cm. (1")

132 B. LITERATURE:
Petrie (1914/1972), no. 35, p. 16, pl. III.

132 C. PAPYRUS SCEPTER AMULET
H. 3 cm. (1 1/8")

132 C. LITERATURE:
Petrie (1914/1972), no. 20, pp. 12-13, pl. II.

132 D. HEART AMULET
H. 2.3 cm. (7/8")

132 D. LITERATURE:
Petrie (1914/1972), no. 7, p. 10, pl. I.

133. EYE OF HORUS PLAQUE
Gold foil over wood
Third Intermediate Period, Dynasty XXI, ca. 1085-945 B.C.
L. 12.7 cm. (5")

133. PROVENANCE:
Ex-collections Drexel, MIA (16.490).

133. COMMENTS:
This Eye of Horus was used to cover the incision wound on a mummy after the viscera had been removed and the wound stitched.

133. PARALLEL:
BMFA 72.4465, *Mummies*, cat. no. 173, p. 222 (metal example).

134 A, B, C

135 A

135 B

136

134. SELECTION OF AMULETS
Glazed faience
Late Period - Ptolemaic Period, 760-30 B.C.

134 A. BABOON
H. 3 cm. (1 1/8")

134 B. HEDGEHOG
L. 2 cm. (13/16")

134 C. SPHINX
H. 2.5 cm. (1")

135. AMULETS
Hematite
New Kingdom - Late Period, Dynasty XVIII-XXXI, ca. 1558-330 B.C.

135 A. TA-WERET
H. 2.5 cm. (1")

135 B. PILLOW
H. 1 cm. (3/8")

137

135 B. LITERATURE:

Petrie (1914/1972), no. 34, p. 15, pl. III.

136. IBIS
Gold
Middle Kingdom, Dynasty XI-XIII, ca. 2040-1633 B.C.
H. 2.2 cm. (7/8")

136. PROVENANCE:

Ex-collections Drexel, MIA (16.470).

136. PARALLEL:

A close parallel in the British Museum is made of electrum and dated to the Middle Kingdom, see Carol A.R. Andrews, *Catalogue of Egyptian Antiquities in the British Museum, VI, Jewellery I*, London, 1981, no. 331, p. 53, pl. 24. An Old Kingdom example is now in Berlin, see Berlin (1967), no. 256, p. 29; and a gold ibis, probably dating to the First Intermediate Period is in the Lowie Museum (6-22885), see Elsasser (1966), p. 58.

137. ANUBIS
Bicolor (blue and pale green)-glazed faience
Late Period - Ptolemaic Period, 760-30 B.C.
Diam. 1.8 cm. (11/16")

138. GRAPE CLUSTER
Glazed faience
New Kingdom, Dynasty XVIII-XX, ca. 1558-1085 B.C.
H. 3.4 cm. (1 3/8")

138

139. NECKLACES
New Kingdom - Late Period, Dynasty XVIII-XXXI, ca. 1558-330 B.C.

139 A. STRING OF AMULETIC AND SPHERICAL BEADS
Carnelian
L. 40 cm. (15 3/8")

139 B. BEADS IN THE FORM OF HORUS THE CHILD
Red, pale blue, and purple-glazed faience
L. 39 cm. (15 3/8")

> **139 B. PROVENANCE:**
>
> Ex-collections Place, MIA (31.50.282).

> **139 B. COMMENTS:**
>
> The color and subject of these beads indicate a manufacture date of late Eighteenth to early Nineteenth Dynasty.

139 C. STRING OF FLOWER BEADS
Multicolor-glazed faience
L. 35 cm. (13 13/16")

> **139 C. COMMENTS:**
>
> The use of multicolored glaze suggests a late Eighteenth Dynasty or Nineteenth Dynasty date for these beads.

139 D. STRING OF COWRIE SHELLS AND BLUE-GLAZED FAIENCE BEADS
L. 39 cm. (15 3/8")

> **139 D. PROVENANCE:**
>
> Ex-collections Place, MIA (31.50.247).

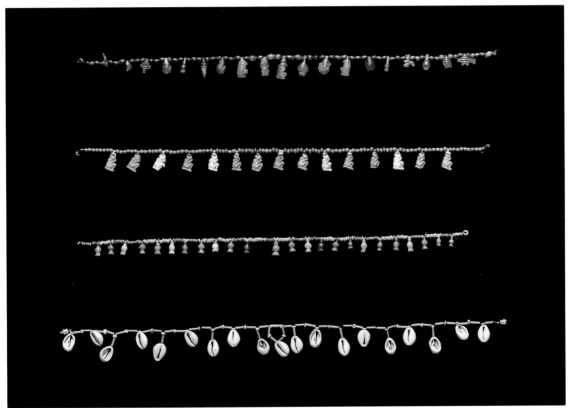

139

140

140. MENAT

Glazed faience
Late Period - Ptolemaic Period, 760-30 B.C.
H. 6.4 cm. (2 1/2")

140. COMMENTS:

The *menat* was used as a counterbalance for heavy necklaces or collars to keep them in place. Collars had a ritualistic or amuletic purpose; the *menat* frequently was decorated with religious or symbolic motifs and also came to acquire its own distinctive, amuletic properties. This example shows a lion-headed aegis crowned with sun disk and uraeus surmounting a rosette.

140. LITERATURE:

Petrie (1914/1972), no. 33, p. 15, pl. III;Reisner (1958), pl. XXIV, nos. 12723, 12721, 12716; Hayes (1959), figs. 153, 164.

141

141. OSIRIS STATUETTE

Bronze
Late Period - Ptolemaic Period, 664-30 B.C.
H. 32 cm. (12 5/8")

141. BIBLIOGRAPHY:
Sotheby's (New York) 20-21 November 1975, lot no. 381.

142. PTAH-SOKAR-OSIRIS FIGURE

Painted gesso over wood
Late Period - Ptolemaic Period, 664-30 B.C.
H. 73.8 cm. (29")

142. COMMENTS:

Ptah-sokar-osiris, a composite deity of resurrection and the afterlife, is represented in this two-figure composition. It shows a mummiform deity wearing a broad collar, full wig, and a headdress that consists of ram's horns, sun disk, and plumes. He faces a mummiform falcon (Sokar). Such images were frequently made to serve as containers for a papyrus or a mummiform "corn mummy," the latter a further symbol of resurrection and rebirth. They were included in private burials from the Late Period to the Ptolemaic Period, although they had been a part of royal burial equipment as early as the New Kingdom. The inscription on the front of this figure is an offering text addressed to Osiris for the benefit of the owner, who is identified as: "Djeher, son of Psamtik and born of Isis-weret." The face is gilt, the remaining decoration being rendered in white, red, yellow, blue, and black paint.

142. PROVENANCE:

Ex-collections Drexel, MIA (16.266).

142. LITERATURE AND PARALLELS:

Mummies, cat. no. 144, p. 197.

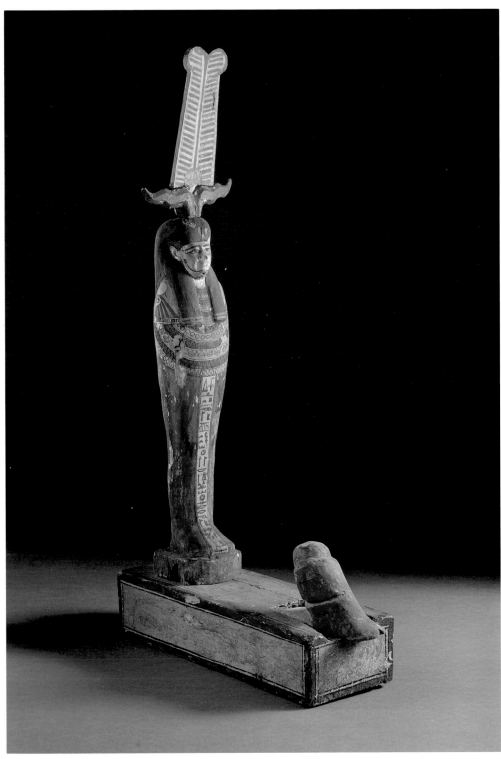

143. MASK FROM A COFFIN LID

Painted wood
Late Period - Ptolemaic Period, 760-30 B.C.
H. 42.1 cm. (l6 5/8")

143

144. MINIATURE CANOPIC JAR
Alabaster
Late Period, Dynasty XXV-XXXI, 760-330 B.C.
H. 24.7 cm. (9 3/4")

144

144. DESCRIPTION:
This miniature canopic vase carries a jackal-head lid.

146

145. DEMOTIC STELA

Sandstone
Ptolemaic Period, 304-30 B.C.
H. 34.3 cm. (13 1/2")

145. PROVENANCE:

Dendara.
Ex-collection Metropolitan Museum of Art (98.4.62).

145. DESCRIPTION:

The round-topped stela shows the mummy of the deceased lying on a lion bed. At either end of the bed, the divine sisters Isis and Nephthys are seated on the ground, their hands raised in a gesture of mourning. Each is identified by her hieroglyphic symbol above the head. Below is a funerary text of four horizontal lines written in Demotic script. It identifies the owner, whose name has been read as Pabekhis.

145. BIBLIOGRAPHY:

W.M.F. Petrie, *Dendereh*, London, 1900, p. 55, no. XIV, pl. XXVA.
Sotheby's (New York) 8-9 February 1985, lot no. 241.

145. LITERATURE AND PARALLELS:

Mummies, cat. no. 186, p. 230.

145. N.B.

The author is grateful to Dr. Robert S. Bianchi, of the Brooklyn Museum, who provided Dr. Harer with bibliographic and background material on this object.

146. STELA OF TSENTWOT

Painted gesso on wood
Ptolemaic Period, 304-30 B.C.
H. 35.6 cm. (14")
W. 30.5 cm.

146. DESCRIPTION:

An elaborate and detailed stela, this example may be divided into four basic zones. The uppermost, the lunette, shows a central winged sun disk, below which is a scarab beetle flanked by a pair of crowned uraeus serpents (Nekhbet and Wadjet) and a similar pair of recumbent jackals (Anubis and Wepwawet). Beneath the lunette, and set off by a *khekher* frieze above and below, is a scene that shows the deceased owner facing a divine boat which carries a complement of deities. The owner raises her hands in adoration and wears a full wig, surmounted by a lotus bud, and a long, full pleated linen gown. Behind her figure is a spiritual aspect of her being represented as a human-headed falcon. The deities on the divine boat may be identified as Khepre (in the form of a scarab in the bow of the vessel), ibis-headed Thoth (Lord of Hermopolis), two female divinities, the falcon-headed sun god Horakhty holding a serpent (Apophis?), two male divinities, and falcon-headed Horus the Elder in the stern. Beneath this zone is the main scene, also set off by a *khekher* frieze. It shows the deceased owner standing, her hands held aloft in adoration of the mummiform god Osiris, his son and wife Horus and Isis, his sister-in-law Nephthys, and jackal-headed Anubis. Below this scene is an hieroglyphic text consisting of six horizontal registers that read right to left. The text registers are alternately painted green and tan, and are set off by blue bands. The entire composition is contained within a *khekher* frieze which is, in turn, encircled by a band of red paint. A palette of white, red, yellow, tan, green, blue, and black was used to create the composition, which blends elements of the solar cult with those of the cult of Osiris.

146. PROVENANCE:

Ex-Pitt-Rivers Collections.

147

148

149

150

147. SHAWABTI FIGURE OF A ROYAL SCRIBE

Painted wood
New Kingdom, Ramesside Period, Dynasty XIX-XX, ca. 1303-1085 B.C.
H. 27.8 cm. (11")

147. PROVENANCE:

Ex-collection Museum of Art and Archaeology, University of Missouri, Columbia.

147. BIBLIOGRAPHY:

Sotheby's (New York) 13 December 1979, lot no. 88.

148. SHAWABTI FIGURE

Terracotta
Second Intermediate Period, Dynasty XIV-XVII, ca. 1786-1558 B.C.
H. 13.3 cm. (5 1/4")

149. SHAWABTI FIGURE OF NAKHT

Painted terracotta
New Kingdom, Ramesside Period, Dynasty XIX-XX, ca. 1303-1085 B.C.
H. 6.3 cm. (2 1/2")

149. PROVENANCE:

Ex-collections Drexel, MIA (16.391).

149. PARALLELS:

Another example is in the Harer Family Trust collection, Ex-MIA 16.390, and it has been reported that two similar figures are in the collection of the Cleveland Museum of Art. See also Newberry (1957), pl. XXXIX, no. 47965.

150. SHAWABTI FIGURE OF THE VICEROY OF NUBIA, HORI I

White-glazed faience
New Kingdom, Dynasty XX, temp. Ramesses III, ca. 1192-1160 B.C.
H. 10.7 cm. (4 1/4")

150. PROVENANCE:

Bubastis, Tomb of Hori I.

150. BIBLIOGRAPHY:

Sotheby's (New York) 13 December 1979, lot no. 85.

150. LITERATURE:

Labib Habachi, *Tell Basta*, Cairo (1957), pp. 100-101, pl. XXXVIIb; Aubert (1974), p. 125, pl. 21, nos. 45-47.

151. SHAWABTI FIGURE OF THE PRIEST OF AMEN, HORI
Blue-glazed faience
New Kingdom, Dynasty XX, ca. 1200-1085 B.C.
H. 12.5 cm. (4 7/8")

151. CONDITION:

Broken and repaired with some restoration.

151. LITERATURE:

See Aubert (1974), pl. 40, figs. 95-96.

152. SHAWABTI FIGURES
Blue-glazed faience
Third Intermediate Period, Dynasty XXI, ca. 1085-945 B.C.

152 A. TAY-WEHERET
H. 10.5 cm. (4 1/8")

152 A. PROVENANCE:

Deir el-Bahari.

152 A. LITERATURE:

See Aubert (1974), pp. 141-143.

152 B. NES-TA-NEB-ISHERU
H. 15 cm. (6 7/8")

152 B. PROVENANCE:

Deir el-Bahari.

152 C. BAK-EN-MUT
H. 9.9 cm. (3 15/16")

152 C. PROVENANCE:

Deir el-Bahari, 1891 (Cache II).

152 C. PARALLELS:

Schneider (1974), no. 4.3.1.18.

152 D. QED-MERIT
H. 9.7 cm. (3 7/8")

152 D. PARALLELS

See Aubert (1974), pl. 51, fig. 120.

151

152 A-D

153. SHAWABTI FIGURE OF GENERAL WEN-DJEBAU-EN-DJED

Bronze
Third Intermediate Period, Dynasty XXI, temp. Psusennes I, ca. 1025 B.C.
H. 8.8 cm. (3 1/2")

153

153. LITERATURE:

See Aubert (1974), pl. 37, fig. 86; Schneider (1977), no. 4.7.11, vol. II, p. 152-153, vol. III, pl. 56.

154. SHAWABTI FIGURE

Blue-glazed faience
Late Period - Ptolemaic Period, ca 760-30 B.C.
H. 12.5 cm. (4 15/16")

154

154. LITERATURE:

For a similar *shawabti* type, see Aubert (1974), pl. 68, fig. 160 and Schneider (1977), no. 5.3.1.115.

ABBREVIATIONS USED IN THE CATALOGUE

Institutional Abbreviations

BM	British Museum
BMFA	Boston Museum of Fine Arts
DREXEL	Drexel Institute, Philadelphia
MIA	Minneapolis Institute of Arts
MMA	Metropolitan Museum of Art
WAG	Walters Art Gallery

Bibliographic Abbreviations

BES	*Bulletin of the Egyptological Seminar*
CG	*Catalogue Général du Musée du Caire*
JARCE	*Journal of the American Research Center in Egypt*
JEA	*Journal of Egyptian Archaeology*

Topographical Bibliography	*Topographical Bibliography of Ancient Egyptian Hieroglyphic Texts, Reliefs and Paintings,* I- VII, Oxford
Berlin (1967)	Kaiser, Werner (ed.). *Agyptisches Museum Berlin.* Berlin, 1967.
du Bourguet (1967)	du Bourguet, Pierre M. *The Art of the Copts.* New York, 1967.
Bourriau (1981)	Bourriau, Janine. *Pottery from the Nile Valley before the Arab Conquest.* Cambridge, 1981.
Bourriau (1988)	Bourriau, Janine. *Pharaohs and Mortals.* Cambridge, 1988.
Brooklyn (1988)	Brooklyn Museum, *Cleopatra's Egypt.* Brooklyn, 1988.
Brooklyn (1989)	Brooklyn Museum, *Ancient Egyptian Art in the Brooklyn Museum.* Brooklyn, 1989.
Chappaz (1984)	Chappaz, Jean Luc. *Les Figurines Funéraires Egyptiennes du Musée d'Art et d'Histoire et de Quelques Collections Privée.* Geneva, 1984.
Ede (1983)	Ede, Charles. *Collecting Antiquities.* London, 1983.
Elsasser (1966)	Elsasser, Albert B. and Vera-Mae Fredrickson, *Ancient Egypt,* Berkeley, 1966.
EGA	Boston Museum of Fine Arts, *Egypt's Golden Age: The Art of Living in the New Kingdom 1558-1085 B.C.* Boston, 1982.
Fazzini (1975)	Fazzini, Richard. *Images for Eternity.* Brooklyn, 1975.
Hayes (1953)	Hayes, William C. *The Scepter of Egypt, Pt. I: From Earliest Times to the End of the Middle Kingdom.* New York, 1953.
Hayes (1959)	Hayes, William C. *The Scepter of Egypt Pt. II: The Hyksos Period and the New Kingdom (1675-1080 B.C.).* New York, 1959.
Hodjash (1982)	Hodjash, Svetlana and Oleg Berlev. *The Egyptian Reliefs and Stelae in the Pushkin Museum of Fine Arts, Moscow.* Leningrad, 1982.
Hoffmann (1988)	Hoffmann, Michael A. *The First Egyptians.* Columbia, SC, 1988.
Kitchen (1982)	Kitchen, K. A. *Pharaoh Triumphant.* Warminster, England, 1982.
Luxor (1979)	Luxor Museum. *The Luxor Museum ofAncient Egyptian Art: Catalogue.* Cairo, 1979.
Matheson (1980)	Matheson, Susan B. *Ancient Glass in the Yale University Art Gallery.* New Haven, 1980.
Mummies (1988)	*Boston Museum of Fine Arts. Mummies and Magic, The Funerary Arts of Ancient Egypt.* Boston, 1988.
Newberry (1957)	Newberry, Percy. *Funerary Statuettes and Model Sarcophagi.* Cairo, 1957.
Patch (1990)	Patch, Diana Craig. *Reflections of Greatness.* Pittsburgh, 1990.
Reisner (1958)	Reisner, George A. *Amulets (CG).* Cairo,1958.
Riefstahl (1968)	Riefstahl, Elizabeth. *Ancient Egyptian Glass and Glazes.* Brooklyn, 1968.
Saleh (1987)	Saleh, Mohamed and Hourig Sourouzian.*The Egyptian Museum Cairo.* Mainz, 1987.
Schimmel	Muscarella, O. W. (ed.) *Ancient Art, The Norbert Schimmel Collection.* Mainz, 1974.

Schneider (1977)   Schneider, Hans D. *Shabtis*, 3 Vols. Leiden, 1977.

Scott (1986)   Scott, Gerry D. III. *Ancient Egyptian Art at Yale*. New Haven, 1986.

Smith (1960)   Smith, William Stevenson. *Ancient Egypt as Represented in the Museum of Fine Arts, Boston*. Boston, 1960.

Spencer (1980)   Spencer, A. J. *Catalogue of Egyptian Antiquities in the British Museum, Vol. VI, Early Dynatic Objects*. London, 1980.

Steindorff (1946)   Steindorff, George. *Catalogue of the Egyptian Sculpture in the Walters Art Gallery*. Baltimore, 1946.

Superior (1978)   Superior Stamp & Coin Co., Inc. *The Sculpture of Ancient Egypt*. Los Angeles, 1978.

Thompson (1982)   Thompson, David L. *Mummy Portraits*. Malibu, 1982.

Vandier d'Abbadie (1972) Vandier d'Abbadie, J. *Catalogue des objets de toilette égyptiens*. Paris, 1972.

Virginia (1973)   Virginia Museum. *Ancient Art in the Virginia Museum*. Richmond, 1973.

Wilkinson (1983)   Wilkinson, Charles K. and Marsha Hill. *Egyptian Wall Paintings, The Metropolitan Museum Collection of Facsimilies*. New York, 1983.